IMAGES
of America

NEBRASKA
BALLROOMS AND
DANCE HALLS

This empty ballroom, likely in the now razed Sheraton-Fontenelle Hotel in Omaha, is a testament to the fate of many such dancing facilities across Nebraska. Most of these grand dance floors have been dormant since the late 1900s, and even more have been destroyed, either by disaster or demolition, throughout the early 2000s. Those that remain active, however, are strong reminders of the period of big band music and its lasting cultural impact upon the state. (Image RP-35mm-4042-002 from the Robert Paskach Collection, donated by Frances Paskach, Michael Paskach, and Karen Givens from the Durham Museum, Omaha, Nebraska. Copyright held by the *Omaha World-Herald*, Omaha, Nebraska.)

ON THE COVER: A couple's dance took place in September 1941 at the Nebraska Chamber of Commerce Building in Lincoln, presently the Lincoln Commercial Club. The venue's high ceilings, extravagant lighting fixtures, grand windows, and impressive balcony made it one of the most popular dance halls in the city. The time on the clock is just after 10:30 p.m., but dances often lasted until midnight or even into the early hours of the morning. (Courtesy of Nebraska State Historical Society Photograph Collections.)

IMAGES
of America

NEBRASKA BALLROOMS AND DANCE HALLS

Austin Truex
Foreword by Mike Flood

ARCADIA
PUBLISHING

Published by Arcadia Publishing
Charleston, South Carolina

Printed in the United States of America

Library of Congress Control Number: 2023946453

For all general information, please contact Arcadia Publishing:
Telephone 843-853-2070
Fax 843-853-0044
E-mail sales@arcadiapublishing.com

Visit us on the Internet at www.arcadiapublishing.com

For Kiley, my dance partner

CONTENTS

FOREWORD

In 2020, the world came face to face with the Covid virus. Businesses closed their doors, people retreated to their homes after being told to quarantine, and hospitals filled to the brim with extremely sick patients. Soon, reports of mass fatalities in our nation's largest cities sent a shock wave of fear across America.

As the owner of radio and television stations in Nebraska, I noticed our customers quickly canceled their advertising because no one was buying cars or walking in the door of their business. In a weird twist of fate, we had no advertisers, but everyone was watching and listening to our stations. Story after story was bad news; people wanted a distraction from everything negative.

On an evening walk, I had the idea to host a live music program that I would call *Quarantine Tonight*. Health officials would only let 10 people gather, which meant it would just be me, the band, and some camera operators. What began in March 2020 would change my life. Harkening back to the early days of radio, my evening show welcomed big bands, polka bands, classic country musicians, pianists, and jazz singers to a program that featured Nebraskans and reminded viewers of watching Lawrence Welk.

Live from our "undisclosed location," Norfolk, Nebraska, VFW Post 1644, each night was a new set of musicians. Days after the program began to air, I started to receive the first of 4,000 handwritten letters from viewers all over Nebraska. *Quarantine Tonight* brought tears to people's eyes as they listened to bands that long ago played at their wedding in some of Nebraska's most historic ballrooms. The bands reminded those over 70 years of age how special their younger years were, dancing in small town ballrooms, finding their first love, and remembering a time that seemed much less complicated.

This book was inspired by the heartfelt memories shared by people from across our state that don't want the happy and special moments that happened in Nebraska's ballrooms to be forgotten by history. Special thanks to Austin Truex for his research and appreciation for the past. I now represent the First District of Nebraska in the US Congress. There are still days where I wish I could be back in front of a band on television with everyone safely tucked into their home and just enjoy two hours of music and good clean entertainment.

This book tells the story of Nebraska ballrooms. It is a story of happiness, talented musicians, and the first time that someone special caught your eye.

—Congressman Mike Flood, First District of Nebraska

ACKNOWLEDGMENTS

First, we must acknowledge everyone who owned, operated, performed at, or danced at ballrooms throughout Nebraska. These people made dancing what it was, and their dedication to the pastime has ensured that ballroom dancing remains an important aspect of our Nebraska culture and history today.

With hundreds of such facilities across the state, this book could never truly include every dance venue, but the hard work of many individuals and organizations made it possible to include many, and I am very thankful. Countless Nebraskan historians and museum volunteers contributed their knowledge and materials. These include folks from the following institutions: the 100th Meridian Museum; the Adams County Historical Society; the Alliance Knight Museum; the Antelope County Museum; the Brown County Historical Society; the Butler County Historical Society; the Cedar County Historical Society; Columbia Hall; the Cuming County Historical Society; the Custer County Museum; the Dakota County Historical Society; the Dawson County Historical Society; the Dixon County Historical Society; the Dodge County Historical Society; the Don O. Lindgren Genealogy Library at the Nebraska Prairie Museum; the Douglas County Historical Society; the Durham Museum; the Great Plains Black History Museum; the Hamilton County Historical Society at the Plainsman Museum; the Harlan County Museum; History Harvest–UNL; the Holt County Historical Society; the Howells Historical Society; Legacy of the Plains–Japanese Hall; the Kansas City Museum in Kansas City, Missouri; the Legacy of the Plains Museum; the Lincoln County Historical Museum; the Merrick County Historical Society; the Nebraska State Historical Society at History Nebraska; the Perkins County Historical Society; the Plains Historical Society; the Sandhills Heritage Museum; the Saunders County Historical Society Museum; the Schuyler Historical Society and Museum; the Scoular Company; the Sioux County Historical Society Museum; the Snyder Firemen's Ballroom; St. Helena Dance Hall; the Stuhr Museum of the Prairie Pioneer; the Thurston County Museum; the Valley County Historical Society; the Webster County Historical Society; West Point Community Theatre; the Wilber Czech Museum; and the Wisner Heritage Museum. Additionally, thank you to the following individuals for providing photographs and information from their personal collections: Jessica Buxton, the Colacino family, Lonny Hansen of the Lonny Lynn Orchestra, Dan Kreikemeier, and Larry Miller. A special thank you to the awesome teams at the Buffalo County Historical Society at the Trails and Rails Museum in Kearney and the University of Nebraska at Kearney History Department, as well as everyone, past and present, at the Elkhorn Valley Museum and Research Center in Norfolk, where my passion for Nebraska history began.

Thank you also to the following newspapers and media organizations and their respective archives for research information: the *Alliance Herald*, the *Alliance Times-Herald*, the *Anselmo Enterprise*, the *Ansley Courier*, the *Ansley Herald*, the *Argosy and the Chronicle-Citizen*, *Arnold Sentinel*, *Aurora News-Register*, the *Banner-Press*, the *Beatrice Daily Express*, *Beatrice Daily Sun*, the *Benson Sun*, *Blaine County Booster*, *Bloomfield Monitor*, the *Blue Hill Leader*, the *Brainard Clipper*, *Brown County Democrat*, *Burt County Herald*, the *Burt County Plaindealer*, *Cedar County News*, *Central City Republican-Nonpareil*,

Central High Register, Chadron Record, Colfax County Call, the Colfax County Press, the Columbus News, the Columbus Telegram, the Commercial Advertiser, the Commercial Advertiser and the Red Cloud Chief, the Comstock News, the Cozad Local, the Creightonian, the Crete News, the Crete Vidette-Herald, the Custer County Chief, the Daily Bulletin, the Daily Democrat, the Dakota County Star, the Dannebrog News, Dawes County Journal, the Decatur Herald, the Dodge Criterion, the Doniphan Enterprise, Dorchester Star, the DuBois Paper, the DuBois Press, Evening World-Herald, the Fairbury Daily News, the Falls City Journal, Flatwater Free Press, Fremont Tribune, the Friend Sentinel, the Frontier and Holt County Independent, the Goldenrod, Gothenburg Independent, the Grand Island Daily Independent, the Grand Island Herald, the Grand Island Independent, the Guide Rock Signal, Harlan County Journal, the Hartington Herald, the Hastings Daily Tribune, the Holdrege Citizen, Holdrege Daily Citizen, the Howells Journal, Humboldt Enterprise, the Independent, the Jewish Press, the Kearney Daily Hub, Kearney Hub, Keith County News, Keloland News, Kenesaw Progress, Legionnaire, the Lexington Clipper and Dawson County Pioneer, Lexington Clipper-Herald, Lincoln County Tribune, Lincoln Farm and Home News, Lincoln Journal Star, Lincoln Nebraska State Journal, the Lincoln Star, the Long Pine Journal, the McCook Daily Gazette, the McCook Gazette, the McCook Republican, the McCook Tribune, the Merrick County Item, the Milligan Review, Mitchell Commercial Tribune, the Morning Spotlight, Nebraska Signal, Neligh News, News-Chronicle, the Niobrara Tribune, Norfolk Daily News, the Norfolk Press, the Norfolk Weekly News-Journal, North Bend Eagle, the North Omaha Sun, the North Platte Semi-Weekly Tribune, the North Platte Telegraph, Omaha Daily Bee, the Omaha Daily News, the Omaha Evening Bee, the Omaha Evening Bee-News, the Omaha Guide, the Omaha Morning Bee-News, the Omaha Star, Omaha World-Herald, the Orchard News, the Ord Quiz, Our Sunday Visitor, Pawnee Republican, the People's Banner, Perkins County Sentinel, Phillips Advertiser, the Phonograph, the Public Mirror, the Randolph Times, the Red Cloud Nation, the Republican-Register, Saline County Journal, the Sargent Leader, the Schuyler Sun, Scottsbluff Daily Star-Herald, Scottsbluff Republican, Seward County Independent, the Sidney News, the Sidney Telegraph, the Snyder Banner, the South Omaha Sun, the Spalding Enterprise, Springview Herald, Star-Herald, the Stuart Advocate, Telegraph-Bulletin, the Times-Tribune, the Tribune-Sentinel, Tri-State Farmer, the Trumpet, the Ulysses Dispatch, the Verdigre Eagle, the Wahoo Democrat, the Wahoo Newspaper, Wayne News, the Western Nebraska Observer, Western Wave, West Point News, the Wilber Republican, the Wymore Arbor State, Yankton Daily Press & Dakotan, and the York Daily News-Times.

Thank you to both Erin Vosgien and Caroline Vickerson at Arcadia Publishing for being so supportive throughout this entire process. Additionally, thank you to Mike Flood, Angie Stenger, and the News Channel Nebraska and Flood Communications teams for all their work supporting this project and for sharing the joy of local music and ballroom dancing through Quarantine Tonight. Additionally, a special thank you to everyone who sent in memories of Nebraska ballrooms to Quarantine Tonight for making this project all the more meaningful.

On a personal note, thank you to my family for their help and support: Aaron, Jessica, Ethan, Jason, Nicole, Brenna, Jacob, and Haidyn, and my grandparents, Nadine and Jean, Barb and Ken, Evaline and Allen, Laurie and Clifford, Mike and Marilyn, and Charles and Thelma. A special shout-out to my grandparents John and Deb for all of their assistance, encouragement, and epic stories. Also, thank you to Orville and Mary Voss for all the work they did during their lives to preserve Norfolk's history. Thank you to Ben Wicker and his family for their generous loan of a scanner for many, many months as well as for the research insights and review that Ben provided. Thank you to Sheryl Schmeckpeper for her guidance and general expertise, as well as her continued work to tell the stories of the Norfolk area. Finally, a massive thank you to my wife, Kiley, for accompanying me on many travels for this project, assisting with extensive research, and supporting me throughout this entire endeavor.

INTRODUCTION

For as long as there have been Nebraskans, there have been Nebraskans looking for somewhere to dance. Dance halls and ballrooms are scattered across the state, from the largest metropolitan centers to the smallest unincorporated communities. Though dancing reached the height of its popularity during the 1940s and 1950s, there are records of dances as far back as the late 1800s. Even in the most sparsely populated areas of Nebraska, there were hundreds of places where people danced throughout the past century. Nebraskans found somewhere to dance wherever they lived, whether that was in stand-alone dance halls, park pavilions, opera houses, the second floors of businesses, homes, barns, gymnasiums, open fields, schools, main streets, theaters, saloons, bars, legion halls, fraternal halls, roller rinks, town halls, community centers, parish halls, country clubs, auditoriums, county fairgrounds, mansions, hotels, or ballrooms. Dances were held wherever space could be found, meaning these buildings often had different primary purposes. Conversely, buildings that were constructed for dancing sometimes held other community events as well. Many of these well-worn structures are now featured in the National Register of Historic Places, highlighting the carefully constructed and beautifully designed halls that exemplify rural living within the state of Nebraska. Throughout different regions of the state, the frequency and styles of dance halls varied, often reflecting the culture and size of the population in the area. Czech, Danish, German, and Japanese groups are only some of those that established dance halls where they settled in Nebraska. These facilities and the people who danced there demonstrate that many diverse groups could all find the good life in Nebraska while still celebrating their cultural heritage.

These structures served as the stage for numerous bands or orchestras playing all sorts of music, and the popularity of ballroom dancing provided a way for even the most rural locales to host larger-than-life legends to perform. The culture of dancing across the state extended beyond the physical building. If there was music playing, there were people there to dance. These two ingredients—people and music—brought ballrooms to life all across Nebraska multiple times a week. As one of the more popular forms of recreation through the mid-1900s, ballroom dancing served a wide range of patrons. Adults spent time together socializing and dancing at these halls. Teens frequented the events, mingling and laughing together. Children attended larger dances and learned from their parents how to participate in the social activity. For band performers, touring around the Midwest was often a way of life, and they regularly trekked through the same circuit of stops in Nebraska. These bands included nationally recognized performers and local artists alike. The famed Lawrence Welk got his start in the Midwest, meaning he performed at numerous locations, small and large, throughout Nebraska both before and after he made it big. Musicians were not the only ones who traveled though, with many groups of dancers driving lengthy distances to either their favorite ballroom or wherever their preferred orchestra was playing. On more than one occasion, these journeys brought two destined strangers together on the dance floor. Many married couples across the state recall falling in love at a ballroom dance, and the small-town connections resulting from this musical happenstance have brought many Nebraskans from different places closer together. In any community, these ballrooms were where people learned both traditional family and innovative modern dances. These dance halls are where people fell in love with someone special, with Nebraska, and with music. These ballrooms were places where Nebraskans gathered to celebrate weddings, anniversaries, fundraisers, presidential birthdays, farewell parties, proms, and, more often than not, nothing at all. These dance halls were places where entire generations grew up.

Today, some ballrooms have been remodeled to serve other purposes, but many have burned down, ending their time as social centers. Despite these changes, there are still a handful of active dance halls in Nebraska, demonstrating that what ballrooms stand for still resonates with people today. These halls are integral to the Nebraska story, and ballroom dancing was an activity that exemplified the rural way of life through recreational connection and community togetherness. After all this time, many ballrooms have faded into the background of our towns, but the memories these dance halls created are bigger than the buildings themselves. Those who were there recollect the sounds of big band music reverberating off the walls, the pounding of feet on a crowded dance floor, and the excited chatter of friends dancing together. The rest of us can only imagine and, if we listen closely enough, hear the musical beats of the ballroom era echoing around us to this day.

One

NORTHEASTERN NEBRASKA

Northeastern Nebraska had a very concentrated number of buildings that were stand-alone dance halls. Because the region was more heavily populated, the density of these ballrooms rarely impacted attendance in a negative way during the height of recreational dancing. Some of the dance halls in this area not explored throughout this chapter include the Cottonwood Inn in Allen; Arlington Ballroom and the Arlington Pavilion in Arlington; King's Dance Pavilion in Blair; the Bloomfield American Legion and Bloomfield Opera House in Bloomfield; Lakeview Pavilion in Brunswick; Center Hall and the Center Parish Hall in Center; the Columbus Armory, the Eagles Club Hall, King's Ballroom, and the Orpheus Opera House in Columbus; Swiss Hall near Columbus; the Constance Auditorium in Constance; the Craig Opera House in Craig; the Crofton Auditorium in Crofton; the Decatur Opera House in Decatur; the TJ Sokol Hall in Dodge; the Knights of Columbus Hall in Elgin; Farmers Club Hall, German Hall, and the Independent Order of Odd Fellows (IOOF) Hall in Emerson; Fordyce Community Hall in Fordyce; the Love-Larson Opera House, Masonic Hall, Morse Park, and the Pathfinder Ballroom in Fremont; the Genoa City Hall in Genoa; the Sun-Glo Ballroom in Hartington; Heun Hall in Heun; the J.C. Bruse Dance Pavilion in Hoskins; the Humphrey Park Ballroom in Humphrey; the Leigh Opera House in Leigh; Lindy Hall in Lindy; the Modern Woodmen of America (MWA) Hall in Martinsburg; Yellow Banks Park near Meadow Grove; the May and Buchholtz Hall and the Morse Bluff Opera House in Morse Bluff; the Green Lantern Dance Hall in Nacora; the Neligh Roller Rink, Riverside Park Pavilion, and Union Hall in Neligh; Highlen's, the Luna Park Dance Pavilion, Marquardt Hall, the Masonic Temple, the Norfolk Country Club, the Trinity Episcopal parish hall, the Union Ballroom, and the Veterans of Foreign Wars (VFW) Hall in Norfolk; Gorey Hall and the North Bend Auditorium in North Bend; the Logan Creek Hall near Oakland; Octavia Hall in Octavia; the Orchard Legion Club in Orchard; Dutch Hall, Farmers Hall, German Hall, and the Pender Legion in Pender; the Pierce Ballroom and the Pierce County Fairgrounds in Pierce; the Red Arrow in Pilger; the Zapadni Cesko Bratrska Jednota (ZCBJ) Hall, also known as Pishelville Hall, in Pishelville; Dufek Dance Pavilion and the Plainview American Legion Club in Plainview; the Sons of Herman Hall in Randolph; Dikeman's Park in Royal; Arroyo's Dance Hall and the Sokol Hall in Schuyler; Ridgely Hall in Scribner; the Tarnov Dance Hall in Tarnov; Tewsville Hall in Tewsville; Logan Hall in Uehling; the Verdel Legion Hall in Verdel; the Waterbury School gym-auditorium, which became Stormin' Norman's Rock 'n' Roll Auditorium, in Waterbury; the Regis Ballroom and the Stratton Hotel in Wayne; Webster Hall in Webster; Koplin's Dance Pavilion in Winside; Dierk's Ballroom, the Land of Nod, Roseland Hall, and the VFW Hall in Wisner; and Homewood Park in Wynot. All these facilities, and more, served the northeastern portion of Nebraska for decades.

The ZCBJ Hall in Niobrara is one of many in Nebraska built by the Western Bohemian Fraternal Association, which is known as the Zapadni Cesko Bratrska Jednota in the original Czech. Operating at a time when some wedding parties invited the entire town to attend, Niobrara's ZCBJ Hall was the venue for a "free wedding dance . . . given by Dean Colwell and Stella" in 1953, which was advertised in the *Niobrara Tribune* and featured music provided by Alice's Orchestra. (Courtesy of the Nebraska State Historical Society Photograph Collections.)

Constructed over 100 years ago in 1913, the St. Helena Dance Hall has hosted a variety of dances for many purposes. Throughout its long tenure, the building has been the site of benefit dances, wedding dances, Halloween dances, and square dances. Recent investment from the community has allowed for renovations to be made to the hall, keeping it active into the present day. (Author's collection.)

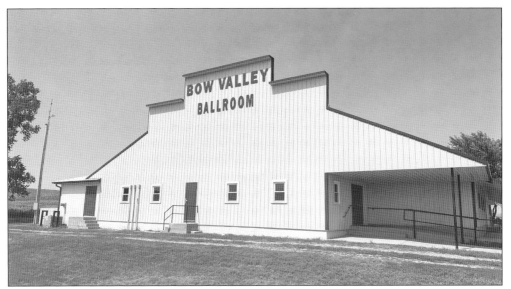

Frequently listed as a busy venue in area newspapers, the Bow Valley Ballroom in Bow Valley was able to draw in large crowds despite its close proximity to other dance halls in the region. Also known as the Bow Valley Hall, the structure has undergone renovations since its initial construction. The *Cedar County News* promoted a dance following a play performance on-site in 1956, and the hall has been the venue for of many weddings. (Author's collection.)

The ZCBJ Opera House in Verdigre served many purposes within the community. A 1917 notice in the *Verdigre Eagle* promoted the "opening dance of the After Lent Season" with music provided by the Pleasant Valley Band. This "first big ball after Lent" demonstrated the impact that religion could have upon dancing as a social event throughout the Midwest. (Courtesy of the Nebraska State Historical Society Photograph Collections.)

The Skylon Ballroom in Hartington has moved locations, although much of the original structure, including the curved roof, is still in place. Well-known throughout the region, the space has been used as a skating rink and dance hall for many years. The ballroom has been the site of various dances, from balls to square dances. (Author's collection.)

From homecoming dances to a Fireman's Ball, the Hartington Auditorium held many receptions within its walls. The scheduled events at the facility often filled up the community's calendar. Dances sponsored by specific businesses provided a method of advertising for the companies, both at the event and in newspapers prior to the occasion. (Author's collection.)

The side of the West Randolph Ballroom promoted it as the place "where the good bands play." In 1939, the *Randolph Times* reported that the ballroom "had a complete sell-out" for its Christmas dance. Such success merited dances to be scheduled for both New Year's Eve and New Year's Day, rather than one or the other, a first for the venue at the time. (Author's collection.)

The Neligh Auditorium, also the town's Independent Order of Odd Fellows (IOOF) Building, held many dances within its walls. The *Neligh News* reported that citizens' reply when approached about purchasing a ticket to a fundraising ball at the auditorium for the volunteer fire department should be "instant and unanimous" since it was the "only time during [the] year support [was] asked" for by the group. Four years later, authorities told the *Neligh News* that a fire in that very auditorium likely occurred because the hall "was being heated in preparation for a dance." (Author's collection.)

The Student Union at Wayne State College, formerly known as the State Normal College and then the State Normal School and Teacher's College, was used for campus activities and dances on a routine basis. The *Goldenrod* campus newspaper reported that when "Steve Reynolds and his band of renowned gentlemen of swing" played at the Student Union following a home game in 1952, everyone was invited to the affair, including all competing speech and debate students from various schools, who were present for the Wayne-hosted Invitational Tourney. (Author's collection.)

The Wayne Auditorium in Wayne hosted to many community events, including a notable dance reported in the *Wayne News* in 1942. When over 80 men from Wayne County were drafted to serve during World War II, the "local chapter of the Legion Auxiliary" hosted a "farewell dance in their honor." The group had initially contemplated gifting "baskets to the boys," but ultimately thought the dance would be more appreciated. (Author's collection.)

The Shady Inn Ballroom was operated by the Peters family as a tavern and dance hall from 1948 through 1957. After the property was sold various times, the facility closed around 1966 or 1967. Located four miles west of Norfolk on Highway 275, the ballroom and adjacent structures have since been demolished. (Courtesy of the Elkhorn Valley Museum and Research Center in Norfolk, Nebraska.)

While open, the Shady Inn Ballroom was a popular joint for residents in the local rural region as well as citizens of Norfolk. Many musical groups performed at the building, ranging from singing to instrumental music. The well-kept and decorated bar offered energetic visitors cold drinks during their breaks from dancing on the polished floor. (Courtesy of the Elkhorn Valley Museum and Research Center in Norfolk, Nebraska.)

King's Ballroom was constructed in Norfolk and opened in 1917. Located near a fork of the Elkhorn River that runs through town, King's Ballroom was severely damaged during a major flood in 1944. The water swept away the entire facility, mostly intact, and it was carried downstream until it got stuck a few blocks away at the Elm Street bridge. Ownership later rebuilt the dance hall. (Courtesy of the Elkhorn Valley Museum and Research Center in Norfolk, Nebraska.)

Seating was available along both sides of the dance floor, which made King's Ballroom a fun venue for children and adults alike. A bar accompanied the adult seating on one side of the floor, while minors filled the other side of the space. Learning specific styles of dancing from adults, including polkas, waltzes, and group dances, kept younger visitors engaged in the fun. (Courtesy of the Elkhorn Valley Museum and Research Center in Norfolk, Nebraska.)

King's Ballroom featured a large wooden dance floor, which was kept pristine even throughout events. During an intermission period, employees would sweep the surface with wide mops while a fresh compound coating was applied to maintain the floor's smooth, glassy appearance. This process granted younger guests the time to play tag until the music and dancing continued. (Courtesy of the Elkhorn Valley Museum and Research Center in Norfolk, Nebraska.)

As one of the most popular dance facilities in northeast Nebraska, King's Ballroom welcomed to several big-name performers of both local and national caliber. Along a hallway in the building hung dozens of posters featuring both previous performers and those to come. When Lawrence Welk performed on-site, the facility reported standing room only. (Courtesy of the Elkhorn Valley Museum and Research Center in Norfolk, Nebraska.)

King's Ballroom featured a windowed pay booth and a coat room. A later addition to the east side of the structure for extra-large crowds became known as the "sheep shed," since it was colder than the rest of the building. Above the dance floor hung a large dome, which was illuminated by spotlights mounted in the ceiling, reflecting a dazzling display across the space. (Courtesy of the Elkhorn Valley Museum and Research Center in Norfolk, Nebraska.)

Beyond public performances, King's Ballroom was also the venue of choice for many personal events, such as weddings or anniversaries. The dance hall was well received by the community, and it remained a popular venue for generations. The ballroom was a regional staple until it met its ultimate end in 1986 in a devastating blaze. (Photograph by Frank Wiedenbach, courtesy of the Reding family.)

Located in downtown Norfolk, Hotel Norfolk was completed in 1926. The building was later renamed Hotel Waldorf and then Hotel Madison. A Hotel Norfolk club dance in 1933, which featured Andy Moats and his Blue Pennant Orchestra, promoted the hotel's ballroom as "cooled with magic weather," referring to air-conditioning, in the *Norfolk Press*. Now known locally as the Kensington Building, the structure is listed in the National Register of Historic Places. (Author's collection.)

Built in the 1930s, the Norfolk City Auditorium was designed to meet the needs of the growing community, and it opened to a crowd of thousands. In 1941, a local school's parent-teacher association discussed utilizing the auditorium to hold dances for the students in the community, with the goal being to make it more difficult for minors to access alcohol. In 1944, Lawrence Welk performed at the facility. (Author's collection.)

Riverside Ballroom in Norfolk was built in the fall of 1936 by the Puschendorf family along the Meridian Highway, presently recognized as Highway 81. The venue, located next to the Elkhorn River, was operated by its founders until 1946, at which point it was sold and later closed. In 2012, the structure was torn down, although the community's memories of the performances, including singers, bands, acrobats, dancers, and magicians, remain. (Courtesy of the Elkhorn Valley Museum and Research Center in Norfolk, Nebraska.)

Riverside Ballroom initially struggled to obtain a loan because of the bleak economic conditions at the time and the perception that such venues were destined to fail. Once it opened, though, dancing proved to be a good outlet for citizens during the Great Depression, as the end of Prohibition also meant the end of speakeasies as popular entertainment spots. Workers and visitors alike enjoyed the ballroom, which could accommodate up to 400 people. (Courtesy of the Elkhorn Valley Museum and Research Center in Norfolk, Nebraska.)

During World War II, tax regulations from the federal government meant Riverside Ballroom could not be publicly open more than twice a week or an additional tax would be applied. This proved not to be a concern, as there were so many private events, such as weddings and farewell parties, during the weekdays that the ballroom maintained activities throughout the entire week without issue, keeping many employed on-site. (Courtesy of the Elkhorn Valley Museum and Research Center in Norfolk, Nebraska.)

Wegner Hall in Wisner was located on the upper floor of a downtown building, shown second from the left in this street scene. Groups from area churches frequently used the space to hold social events, which included card games, raffles, and dances. The local paper, the *News-Chronicle*, mentions that "benefit card parties" typically included dancing, often with the Venjohn brothers furnishing the music, sometimes as a donation. (Courtesy of the Wisner Heritage Museum.)

In years past, the Beemer Ballroom was the venue for dances of varying purposes, including volunteer fire department benefit dances, wedding dances, Easter dances, and polio benefit dances, among others. Monthly schedules for the ballroom released in the *Dodge Criterion* were often packed full of events for those both in town and in the surrounding communities to enjoy. (Author's collection.)

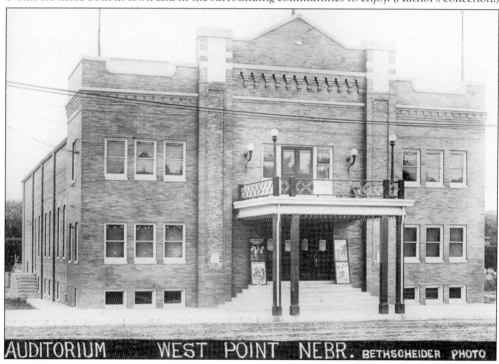

West Point's auditorium was a very busy location for both dances and other events. As with many other small communities, the building served a variety of functions for the town. A benefit for the West Point Memorial Hospital was held at the auditorium in 1950, offering attendees a dance as well as a meal and other entertainment. (Author's collection.)

Located in rural Burt County, the community of Bertha was home to the Bertha Ballroom, also known as Bertha Hall. Although its present-day appearance may indicate otherwise, the facility attracted up to 600 dancers from miles away back in its heyday, when performers like Lawrence Welk and Dick DeFord played music on-site. Bertha Hall was reportedly one of the earliest structures in the area to get electricity. (Author's collection.)

It took over two years to construct the Tekamah Auditorium, which was funded in part through the Works Progress Administration. When the building was completed in 1938, the opening ball attracted a reported 2,000 people from a variety of communities both near and far. The installed dance floor was designed to accommodate 750 couples and was certainly broken in at the initial celebration. (Author's collection.)

In 1934, the original Howells Ballroom opened with a completely packed audience of dancers. Some reports cite as many as 3,000 attendees at the ballroom's inaugural night. The facility had its beginnings as an outdoor venue as early as 1931 until local demand and repeated battles with poor weather necessitated an enclosed dance hall. (Courtesy of the Howells Historical Society.)

The old Howells Ballroom originated with the Howells Volunteer Fire Department. The group often hosted community dances, and the desire for a permanent venue resulted in the construction of the Howells Ballroom. The new facility attracted significant talent in bands and orchestras that came to perform, with all proceeds going toward the fire department. (Courtesy of the Howells Historical Society.)

At its peak, the first Howells Ballroom drew in big-name performers, including Lawrence Welk. Crowded Sunday evening dances led the facility to become regionally popular, earning a reputation as the dance center of northeast Nebraska within many circles. Such traffic resulted in profit, enabling the structure to be updated as time progressed. (Courtesy of the Howells Historical Society.)

Decades after the old Howells Ballroom was completed, the new Howells Ballroom was built in 1964. In contrast to the original primarily wooden structure, the new ballroom was constructed using steel. The ballroom's massive dance floor is 5,000 square feet. With capacity for 700 people within the building, the Howells Ballroom remains an active asset within the community. (Courtesy of the Howells Historical Society.)

Howells was also the site of Bohemian National Hall. As it would in later years with the ever-popular Howells Ballroom, the community often rallied around dances held at the Bohemian National Hall. Newspaper advertisements in the *Howells Journal* often stated that "everybody [was] invited," a window into the strong fellowship that bound communities together. (Courtesy of the Nebraska State Historical Society Photograph Collections.)

The ZCBJ Opera House in Clarkson was built in 1915. Doubling as Clarkson's dance hall, the opera house hosted bands from a variety of locations, including Omaha's Golden Prague Orchestra, which the *Colfax County Press* praised for playing "Old Time, Bohemian, German, and Modern Music." Dances at the venue were often sponsored by the local ZCBJ lodge. (Author's collection.)

The iconic Firemen's Ballroom in Snyder has been operated by the Snyder Volunteer Fire Department since the facility was constructed in 1930. The ballroom has had hundreds of well-attended events, including wedding dances, holiday dances, and community dances. The *Snyder Banner* wrote in 1939 that the facility provided dancers with "the best in music [and] the best floor." Notable performers included Lawrence Welk in 1934, Les's Merry Men Orchestra in 1954, and the Glen Bowman Orchestra in 1964. (Courtesy of Dan Kreikemeier and the Snyder Firemen's Ballroom.)

North Bend's Modern Woodsmen of America (MWA) Hall was constructed by the group's local chapter. The *North Bend Eagle* advertised that the space was used as the venue for a "public St. Patrick's Day dance" on the date of the holiday in 1932 as well as for a "Royal Neighbor dance" in 1933, at which a meal was served and some locals showcased specific dance numbers to attendees. (Author's collection.)

The Municipal Auditorium in Fremont frequently hosted to large-scale community activities such as dances. In 1946, the *Fremont Tribune* recorded a request from the local Junior Chamber of Commerce for a curfew of 1:00 a.m., rather than the usual midnight, for auditorium dances in order "to meet competition of surrounding cities and keep Fremont young people at home." The city council, finding no recorded policy that midnight was the required curfew, swiftly passed a unanimous motion to set the midnight curfew as law, being commended by the Fremont Ministerial Association for doing so and not permitting later dancing. (Author's collection.)

The Oak Ballroom in Schuyler proved to be so popular the managers of the dance hall would have to use innovative methods to keep events feeling new. One such instance was a Battle Dance sponsored by the fire department on Halloween in 1946, which involved two bands performing simultaneously at opposite ends of the dance floor in an attempt to outplay the opposition and retain most of the dancers on their end of the hall. (Courtesy of the Schuyler Historical Society.)

Schuyler's Oak Ballroom takes its name from "the huge natural oak timbers and beams cut from the native oak trees in Butler County and Shell Creek precinct of Colfax County" that were used to construct the facility. These resources, paired with "native rock for [the] walls and foundation," gave the facility strong local roots, which a 1997 story in the *Schuyler Sun* reflected upon. (Courtesy of the Schuyler Historical Society.)

The Oak Ballroom took two years to build and was completed in 1937. The dedication ceremony saw the ever-popular Lawrence Welk and his orchestra visit Schuyler to perform for the occasion. The total expense for the project, which was completed through the Works Progress Administration, was $37,000. (Author's collection.)

Schuyler's Czech-Slovak Protective Society (CSPS) Hall often encouraged dancing as a pastime for members of the town. The fraternal organization offered the community lessons in tap dancing and ballroom dancing. An advertisement in the *Schuyler Sun* promised "one free pancake lunch with each dance ticket" for a "pancake dance" at the CSPS Hall. (Courtesy of the Schuyler Historical Society.)

The ZCBJ Hall in Schuyler was earlier called the CSPS Hall. The transition took place following a larger regional trend in Czech settlements, in which the CSPS organizations became ZCBJ groups, so their buildings were renamed accordingly. Although the name did change, the dancing that occurred at the facility did not. The building was the site of ZCBJ party dances for anyone who wished to attend. (Courtesy of the Schuyler Historical Society.)

The Linwood ZCBJ Hall was another site built by those with a Czech background. Now overrun with trees and bushes, the building was originally constructed to be used for events like a 1939 dance with an appearance by the Pabian Orchestra. A 1981 Rural Fire Protection District annual dance held at the Linwood ZCBJ Hall featured Bob Blecha and His Bouncing Czechs. (Author's collection.)

The ZCBJ Hall in Morse Bluff was built in 1911. Now listed in the National Register of Historic Places, the building is also presently operated by the local American Legion Post 340. Throughout these groups' tenures, the hall has also been the site of community dances, wedding receptions, and private events, including a dance to celebrate a local couple's 25th wedding anniversary in 1960. (Courtesy of the Nebraska State Historical Society Photograph Collections.)

Duncan's Pulaski Hall, still in operation today, has an extensive history of dances and community events. In 1941, the Duncan Volunteer Fire Department hosted an Iron Lung Benefit Dance at Pulaski Hall, with Duffy Belohrad's Accordion Band playing. While the proceeds may now go to different causes, benefit dances are not uncommon at a modern-day dance hall. (Author's collection.)

Founded as the TJ Sokol Hall in 1923 and now known as the Abie Auditorium, this dance facility proved to be a popular venue around World War II. The local lodge had once been in a small building nearby, but after it moved to the larger auditorium, the community of Abie often hosted upwards of 800 attendees for public dances. One such event, a four-hour-long New Year's Eve dance, featured the Michael Brecka Orchestra. (Author's collection.)

Two

OMAHA

As the largest metropolitan community in Nebraska, Omaha had significantly more dance halls than other communities, including Lincoln. Dominated by neighborhood park pavilions, massive hotels with equally impressive ballrooms, and stand-alone dance halls, Omaha was a prime example of what ballroom dancing culture looked like throughout the mid- to late 1900s. Nearly every community within Omaha had some form of dance site, and the cultural differences within the same city were magnified by the variation in music played and performers recruited, although there was certainly overlap as well. Some of the facilities found throughout Omaha and its surrounding communities that are not examined in the upcoming pages include Harte's Hall in Dundee; Linoma Beach near Gretna; the Acme Hotel-Bar, the Brown Park Pavilion, the Castle Hotel Ballroom, the Catholic Sokol Hall, Crown Hall, Dannebrog Hall, the Elks Club Hall, the Field Club Dancing Pavilion, Firefighters Union Hall, the Fontenelle Park Pavilion, the Idle-Wilde Hall, the Masonic Temple, the Millrose Ballroom, the Orpheum Dance Hall, the Seymour Lake Club, the South Omaha Sokol Hall, the VFW Hall, and Washington Hall in Omaha; Bushwackers Dance Hall and Saloon and the Lakoma Country Club in Ralston; and the Springfield Community Hall in Springfield. These venues, along with dozens of others, make Omaha the capital of Nebraska dancing facilities.

The new Riverview Park Pavilion in Omaha opened in 1950, costing $75,000. The dedication dance for the pavilion, publicized in the *Evening World-Herald* and hosted by the Park and Recreation Commission, included a "free polka party open to the public," with the Rudy Vell orchestra furnishing the melodies. The dance pavilion had space for 600 people—400 indoors and 200 out on the veranda. (Courtesy of the Nebraska State Historical Society Photograph Collections.)

The Carter Lake Dance Hall in Omaha, also known as the Carter Lake Club Dance Pavilion, was home to the Carter Lake Dancing Club, which often hosted dances, although advertisements in the *Omaha World-Herald* made it clear that it was common for "only couples [to be] admitted." In 1936, the *Omaha Evening Bee-News* reported that the pavilion was damaged when an "84-mile-an-hour wind" toppled a massive tree onto the structure. (Image BF507-052 from the Bostwick-Frohardt Collection, owned by KM3TV and on permanent loan to the Durham Museum, Omaha, Nebraska.)

The Elmwood Park Pavilion in Omaha is another outdoor dance facility. Many parks throughout the state, and within larger cities in particular, provided a pavilion for public use, whether that be for picnics, parties, or dances. As recorded in the *Omaha Evening Bee* in 1936, the Elmwood Park Pavilion was the location where, "for the first time since its organization, the federal music project . . . played for dancing" following a concert performance. The dance was so well received that it inspired additional public dances with the musical ensemble performing. (Courtesy of the Douglas County Historical Society of Omaha, Nebraska.)

Omaha's Benson Park Pavilion served as a dance pavilion for one of the most populated regions in the state. Many of the dances held there were for square dancing specifically, which necessitated a designated person to call out the dance moves. At the Benson Park Pavilion, Fred Ehlers, Glenn Lapham, and Don Gammel were just some of the folks who served as callers to help square dancing run smoothly. (Courtesy of the Douglas County Historical Society of Omaha, Nebraska.)

The Miller Park Pavilion in Omaha proved to be an excellent venue for youth dances. After a 1920 dance, the *Omaha World-Herald* printed a city official's report that "some of the young folks got a little free, but . . . on the whole it was O. K." The positive feedback encouraged officials to permit additional dances for youth at the pavilion. (Courtesy of the Douglas County Historical Society of Omaha, Nebraska.)

The Miller Park Pavilion in Omaha continued to be an active venue throughout the years, and even as modes of transportation evolved, folks found their way to the local dance hall. Various clubs held events on-site, including a dance in 1958 when the *Evening World-Herald* reported that "the Fairs and Squares and [the] Allemande Thor Square Dance Clubs" would share hosting duties. Only a few years later, in 1962, the Benson Sun noted that the Fairs and Squares Square Dance Club had partnered with the Twirl 'N' Whirl Merry Mixers to host a dance at the pavilion. (Image BF7-526 from the Homer O. Frohardt Collection, from the Durham Museum, Omaha, Nebraska.)

The Hanscom Park Pavilion of Omaha was once under consideration to be the location of municipal dances. The *Omaha Daily Bee* described a section of the original structure's higher level that was "without walls" and had "a wide porch extending around the four sides of the building," providing ample room for dancers. The pavilion burned down in 1927 and was replaced shortly thereafter. (Image HOFP-221 from the Homer O. Frohardt Collection of the Durham Museum, Omaha, Nebraska.)

Omaha's Krug Park Danceland was a very popular dancing spot in the region. As a part of a larger amusement park, it was nearby other recreational facilities. Many advertisements in newspapers such as the *Evening World-Herald* encouraged readers to "arrange [their] dancing parties" on-site. The facility was also known as the Krug Park Ballroom, the Krug Park Dance Hall, or the Krug Park Dance Pavilion. (Courtesy of the Douglas County Historical Society of Omaha, Nebraska.)

Krug Park's Dance Hall was often very crowded at the height of its popularity. Despite being one of the largest dance halls in Nebraska, with room for over 1,000 couples, the frequent recruitment of the best bands in the Midwest consistently kept the ballroom operating at capacity. As the *Omaha World-Herald* put it, the dance hall had a "strict policy of dance supervision," which ensured that unruly dancers were swiftly removed. (Image WW127-003 from the Permanent Collection of the Durham Museum, Omaha, Nebraska.)

Krug Park's Danceland in Omaha was noted to have "the best Dance Floor it was possible to lay," making it a well-attended facility, even by the standards of the largest city in the state. The *Evening World-Herald* described the dance floor as impeccably maintained, consisting of "two-inch maple flooring, dressed down to a smoothness of glass." (Image BF26-202 from the Bostwick-Frohardt Collection, owned by KM3TV and on permanent loan to the Durham Museum, Omaha, Nebraska.)

Dozens of different bands and performers frequented the Krug Park Dance Pavilion throughout the years. Eddie Jungbluth's Orchestra was a well-known group that played a long-term contract at the venue. The LeRoy Smith 12-Piece Orchestra, which the *Evening World-Herald* deemed "second to none in the state," also appeared at the site. (Image BF5645-004 from the Bostwick-Frohardt Collection, owned by KM3TV and on permanent loan to the Durham Museum, Omaha, Nebraska.)

Krug Park Ballroom met its end in 1944, when the building burned down, much like many other dance halls across Nebraska and the country at large. When the inferno destroyed the building, it was the only facility at the old Krug Park complex still in operation. The *Omaha World-Herald* reported that "hundreds of motorists jammed streets" around the park to see the blaze and the damage to the ballroom, "despite gasoline rationing" at the time. (Image JS1A-020 from the John S. Savage Collection, from the Durham Museum, Omaha, Nebraska. Copyright held by the *Omaha World-Herald*, Omaha, Nebraska.)

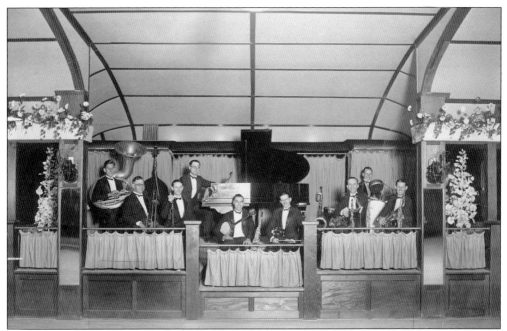

The Royal Terrace Ballroom could be found on the grounds of Peony Park, an amusement park in Omaha. The Royal Terrace Ballroom had many loyal regulars. A 1925 *Omaha Daily Bee* advertisement highlighting the sources of the facility's popularity praised its "properly conducted and supervised [dances], polite service, and . . . beautiful ball room." The same advertisement also credited the Ed Meyers orchestra as a reason dancers enjoyed themselves. (Image BF2299-005 from the Bostwick-Frohardt Collection, owned by KM3TV and on permanent loan to the Durham Museum, Omaha, Nebraska.)

Despite its popularity, the Royal Terrace Ballroom did face challenges. In 1925, the building burned down, leaving the owners with a complete loss of the facility. The Malec brothers, who owned much of the larger Peony Park property, wasted no time building this improved dance hall to succeed the structure. (Image BF2299-013 from the Bostwick-Frohardt Collection, owned by KM3TV and on permanent loan to the Durham Museum, Omaha, Nebraska.)

Mere months after the original ballroom at Peony Park went up in flames, Omaha celebrated the opening of the new dance hall replacing it. The *Omaha World-Herald* promoted the "70x112 feet dance floor, free of posts." The owners of the hall emphasized that "the frame structure" that had been destroyed was being "replaced with a real brick building" to offer customers a better dance hall and experience. (Image 1994-65-52-896 from the Permanent Collection of the Durham Museum, Omaha, Nebraska.)

The Royal Terrace Ballroom in Omaha brought hundreds of Nebraskans to the facility to both listen to and dance to music. In addition to the ballroom dancing indoors, dances also took place at Peony Park's outdoor pavilion, called the Royal Grove, which drew impressive crowds during the warmer months. There were also other features to the amusement park, including a pool and various rides. (Image 1994-65-52-362 from the Permanent Collection of the Durham Museum, Omaha, Nebraska.)

The Royal Terrace Ballroom at Peony Park often brought in top talent from the world of big band music. In 1958, the *Omaha World-Herald* advertised that Woody Herman and his "famous Third Herd recording and TV dance orchestra" would be performing at the venue. On another occasion, Lambert Bartak (left), the well-known Nebraskan organist, appeared on-site to play accordion for a dance. (Image 1994-65-52-984 from the Permanent Collection of the Durham Museum, Omaha, Nebraska.)

Although commonly known as the Royal Terrace Ballroom, the Omaha dance hall was also called other titles. These included the Peony Park Ballroom or the Peony Park Dance Hall. Peony Park, although the name of the entire amusement park, was often used synonymously with the dance hall on the grounds. (Image 1994-65-52-1182 from the Permanent Collection of the Durham Museum, Omaha, Nebraska.)

Already having faced forced changes due to the 1925 fire, the Royal Terrace received another remodel in 1940. The *Omaha World-Herald* reported that "the entire floor of the ballroom was lowered" and "new railings, over a mile of new carpeting, new bandstand equipment, and new fluorescent lighting" were components of the project. The "new Peony terrace" looked fresh and was more technically capable of continuing to entertain Omaha. (Image 1994-65-52-339 from the Permanent Collection of the Durham Museum, Omaha, Nebraska.)

Omaha's Royal Terrace Ballroom was big enough to accommodate large organizations, such as the Shriners at this 1960 dance. Later, when some other ballrooms in Nebraska had already started to decline in popularity, the Royal Terrace often maintained decently sized crowds for dances. Despite late successes, the dance hall closed its doors for good in 1994. (Image JS5EE-113 from the John S. Savage Collection, from the Durham Museum, Omaha, Nebraska. Copyright held by the *Omaha World-Herald*, Omaha, Nebraska.)

Omaha's Royal Terrace had something that many notable ballrooms at the time also had—a ticket booth. Admission to get into dances varied depending upon the location, the purpose of the event, and the band that was performing. Many larger dance halls would also offer a coat check for attendees. (Image 1994-65-52-1185 from the Permanent Collection of the Durham Museum, Omaha, Nebraska.)

The Joslyn Castle in Omaha is a well-known landmark within Nebraska's metropolis and has been since its construction in 1903. The incredible mansion is a prime example of what only a small percentage of Nebraskans could do—have a ballroom in their own home. Joslyn Castle's ballroom would have been used as a dedicated entertainment space. Many Nebraskans would hold dances in their homes, but few had a literal ballroom in which to do so. (Author's collection.)

The Omaha Scottish Rite Cathedral was typically the site of dances held by specific clubs. These classy dance groups included the Cinosam Dancing Club and the Crescent Formal Dancing Club, both of which held various dancing parties at the venue and notified members of such occasions through notices in newspapers like the *Evening World-Herald*. (Author's collection.)

The Omaha Sokol Auditorium could be found at the intersection of Thirteenth and Martha Streets, and it was often the site of public dances for the metropolitan community. The original structure, seen here, was replaced in the 1920s. In 1962, the *Omaha World-Herald* informed readers that the auditorium was to host the "World Famous Radio and TV Stars, [the] Six Fat Dutchmen," a popular musical group from the era. (Image BF2331-062 from the Bostwick-Frohardt Collection, owned by KM3TV and on permanent loan to the Durham Museum, Omaha, Nebraska.)

The Blackstone Hotel Ballroom in Omaha featured multiple dancing clubs in its day. The local Holiday Club occasionally held dinner dances at the venue. In 1959, the *Evening World-Herald* posted a notice that the Soiree Club's "Tenth Anniversary Dance" would be at the Blackstone Hotel Ballroom. These dancing groups kept many Omaha ballrooms, particularly within hotels, busy throughout the year. (Author's collection.)

Like many other groups, the dancing clubs based out of the Blackstone Hotel in Omaha often recruited talent to attract attendees for events. Here, Hildegarde Loretta Sell, a cabaret singer, performs at the Blackstone Hotel Ballroom for a festive occasion. Specific singers and bands, particularly those who were in high enough demand to be traveling throughout the region, often drew in larger crowds. These exclusive performances were popular with local dancers. (Image JS30A-021H from the John S. Savage Collection, from the Durham Museum, Omaha, Nebraska. Copyright held by the *Omaha World-Herald*, Omaha, Nebraska.)

The Blackstone Hotel Ballroom in Omaha proved to be a versatile space for functions throughout the years, often featuring dances for a variety of organizations and holidays. In 1952, the Cornell University Ball, seen here, was held in the ballroom, and in 1953, it was the site of a Mardi Gras Ball. (Image JS30B-041S from the John S. Savage Collection, from the Durham Museum, Omaha, Nebraska. Copyright held by the *Omaha World-Herald*, Omaha, Nebraska.)

In 1935, the Blackstone Hotel Ballroom hosted a lively "costume masquerade party" put on by the Junior Dundee Dancing Club. The *Omaha Evening Bee-News* provided a roster of the winners of specific categories, including an "old-fashioned hooped gown" that took first prize, an aviator outfit that was the "best character costume," and two cousins in genuine Scottish attire who won "best pair." (Image BF1798-052 from the Bostwick-Frohardt Collection, owned by KM3TV and on permanent loan to the Durham Museum, Omaha, Nebraska.)

Across the entire state of Nebraska and particularly within metropolitan cities, many hotels provided spaces for larger events. Within Omaha, the Diplomat Hotel's Ballroom was one of these venues. Utilized by community members and visitors alike, these hotel ballrooms often hosted dances, receptions, conferences, or banquets. Many clubs would hold dances in the space, including the La Salle Dance Club and the Welcome Wagon Club. (Courtesy of the Douglas County Historical Society of Omaha, Nebraska.)

The Conant Hotel Ballroom in Omaha was occasionally the site of private events. In 1929, the *Omaha Evening Bee-News* published a story covering a "private supper-dance" for around 100 people at the Conant Hotel Ballroom. The event was to take place on Halloween night, and "the dancing party" was hosted by a Mr. and Mrs. Leon Millard. (Image BF1390-012 from the Bostwick-Frohardt Collection, owned by KM3TV and on permanent loan to the Durham Museum, Omaha, Nebraska.)

The Fontenelle Hotel in Omaha opened in 1915, and its ballroom was once considered to be one of the finest social centers in the city. A dance on-site, the theme of which was very secretive, was put together by a Mr. and Mrs. Hoxie Clark who had been visiting Omaha. Three different local dance clubs were invited, all of whom had at one point entertained the couple while they were in town. (Image BF506-389 from the Bostwick-Frohardt Collection, owned by KM3TV and on permanent loan to the Durham Museum, Omaha, Nebraska.)

The Logan Hotel in Omaha also offered a dancing space for locals. An advertisement in the *Omaha World-Herald* promoted "The South Sea Island Room," which was an accordingly decorated dance floor. Bands like Randall's Royals played at the venue, where a mezzanine floor meant the music was heard on multiple levels in the hotel. (Image WW36-003 from the Permanent Collection of the Durham Museum, Omaha, Nebraska.)

Hotel Rome, Omaha, Neb.

The Hotel Rome Ballroom in Omaha frequently promoted the big dances it hosted for community members. In 1923, the *Jewish Press* reported that the New Year's Eve dance at the ballroom would last until 3:00 a.m. the following morning and that "everybody [would] be there." Wilderman's Orchestra provided the music for the celebration. (Author's collection.)

Omaha's Paxton Hotel Ballroom was frequently the site of supper-dances, at which hosts would treat guests to a meal and a dance. These popular social events ranged in size, but the overarching idea was made clear in the *Legionnaire* newspaper: "dine and dance." In the hotel's ballroom, nicknamed "the Pax Room," there was often "dancing every night but Sunday," as was common for many dance halls across Nebraska. (Courtesy of the Nebraska State Historical Society Photograph Collections.)

The Omaha Civic Auditorium was a dance facility that featured some hugely famous performers in its day. At what was billed by the *Omaha World-Herald* as "the largest in-person show of '56," musicians like Ella Johnson, Bill Haley and the Comets, and Chuck Berry made appearances. Nine years later, in 1965, the *South Omaha Sun* advertised that James Brown would soon hold a dance and show at the auditorium. (Image BF611-004 from the Bostwick-Frohardt Collection, owned by KM3TV and on permanent loan to the Durham Museum, Omaha, Nebraska.)

The Civic Auditorium in Omaha held a variety of dances. In 1965, the *South Omaha Sun* publicized an upcoming square dance hosted by the Omaha Area Square Dance Callers Association. As with many facilities, one did not have to actually dance to partake in the social gathering at the Civic Auditorium. The same advertisement noted that "spectators [were] welcome" at the dance. (Image BF611-002 from the Bostwick-Frohardt Collection, owned by KM3TV and on permanent loan to the Durham Museum, Omaha, Nebraska.)

Omaha's Happy Hollow Club was originally located in this building. While a country club, dances at this facility were frequent, and lists of attendees were often posted in the newspaper afterwards. Specifically, dinner dances proved to be popular, attracting many guests to the Happy Hollow Club with the promise of both a delicious meal and a good time. (Author's collection.)

The Happy Hollow Club in Omaha later moved to a different location, and dances remained popular at the new facility. In 1950, this season-opening dance in the Happy Hollow Club's ballroom attracted a large crowd. The establishment continued holding events throughout the years, including "informal dinner-dance[s] for members," as the *Omaha World-Herald* reported in 1961. (Image JS5A-136 from the John S. Savage Collection, from the Durham Museum, Omaha, Nebraska. Copyright held by the *Omaha World-Herald*, Omaha, Nebraska.)

Presently named Brownell-Talbot, Brownell Hall in Omaha was originally a girls' boarding school. In 1923, the school moved into what was formerly the original Happy Hollow Club building. The school hosted a yearly Christmas holiday dance in the gymnasium, like this 1938 occasion, carrying on the legacy of ballroom dancing in the clubhouse. (Image BF19-254 from the Bostwick-Frohardt Collection, owned by KM3TV and on permanent loan to the Durham Museum, Omaha, Nebraska.)

Like other clubs in the city, the Omaha Country Club was a venue often used by members to entertain guests. Local residents would host out-of-town visitors in their homes for a meal preceding a larger dance gathering with others at the country club facility. These instances were once newsworthy enough to make the daily paper. (Image BF51-138 from the Bostwick-Frohardt Collection, owned by KM3TV and on permanent loan to the Durham Museum, Omaha, Nebraska.)

Originally utilized by the Knights of Ak-Sar-Ben, the Aksarben Ballroom was another dancing facility located in Omaha. The ballroom itself was found within the Ak-Sar-Ben Den. Once the primary location for the organization's pageants and community gatherings, the original facility was destroyed in a 1927 blaze. Here, the space is decorated in preparation for a yearly event. (Courtesy of Douglas County Historical Society.)

Although the Aksarben Ballroom burned down, the organization continued to host fundraisers, galas, and balls at the Aksarben Coliseum in Omaha. A 1941 Coronation Ball crowned Alice Meyer as Aksarben queen. The event, which has long been a fundraiser for Aksarben and still occurs today, recognizes Nebraskans for volunteerism, philanthropy, and dedication to community service. (Image JS3B-116 from the John S. Savage Collection, from the Durham Museum, Omaha, Nebraska. Copyright held by the *Omaha World-Herald*, Omaha, Nebraska.)

The Knights of Columbus Hall in Omaha was constructed in 1927, and it was one of the largest buildings utilized for volunteer and social work in town at the time. Eventually changing hands to become Nebraska's American Legion Hall No. 1, the structure's ballroom was active throughout both groups' times using the facility, hosting dances and balls of all sorts. (Image BF647SS-064 from the Bostwick-Frohardt Collection, owned by KM3TV and on permanent loan to the Durham Museum, Omaha, Nebraska.)

In 1987, the Scoular Company purchased what was once the Knights of Columbus Hall to be used as business offices. The company took care to both renovate and restore the historic structure, bringing the ballroom back into operation since owners of the building after the American Legion had not been as active in the space. The Scoular Ballroom was then used for dances once again, such as the 1992 South High School prom. (Image BF2673-008 from the Bostwick-Frohardt Collection, owned by KM3TV and on permanent loan to the Durham Museum, Omaha, Nebraska.)

With roots dating back to 1936, the Music Box was a staple in Omaha's arts and entertainment scene for decades. The Music Box was the show venue for many big-name performers, even as early as 1938, when the *Evening World-Herald* reported that Wally Stoefler and his NBC Orchestra was to play on-site. The ballroom had to undergo repairs following a fire in 1951. (Courtesy of the Douglas County Historical Society of Omaha, Nebraska.)

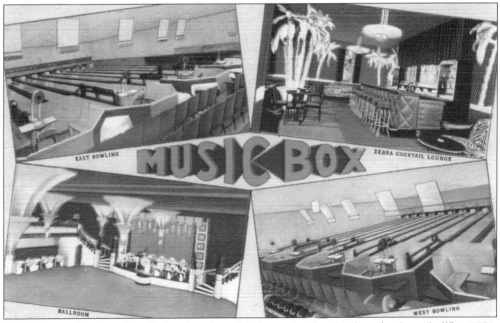

In later years, the Music Box declined in the public's eye. A police "raid on the dance hall" in 1971, covered extensively by the *Omaha World-Herald*, led to 19 minors being arrested and the end of youth dances at the venue, following a number of concerns and complaints about what went on at the facility. (Courtesy of the Douglas County Historical Society of Omaha, Nebraska.)

The Deluxe Ballroom in Omaha, home to the Deluxe Dancing Academy, operated for a number of years in the early 1900s. The facility held both dance classes and regular dances for the public. In 1916, a weekly schedule in the *Omaha Evening Bee* stated that school took place Monday and Wednesday evenings, while public dances were Tuesday, Thursday, Saturday, and Sunday nights. (Image BF693-003 from the Bostwick-Frohardt Collection, owned by KM3TV and on permanent loan to the Durham Museum, Omaha, Nebraska.)

The Rose Bowl Ballroom in Omaha, formerly the Deluxe Ballroom, attracted large dance crowds. Although there are only records of the renamed dance hall operating in the year 1938, there were numerous dances held there, including one on New Year's Eve, for which the *Omaha World-Herald* promoted "moderate prices, free hats, [and] noisemakers." (Image BF5675-001 from the Bostwick-Frohardt Collection, owned by KM3TV on permanent loan to the Durham Museum, Omaha, Nebraska.)

The popular Dreamland Ballroom was found within the Jewell Building in Omaha. It was built, owned, and operated by the Jewell family, Black entrepreneurs who were looking to establish an entertainment venue for the neighborhood. The building had the Dreamland Ballroom on the second floor and a pool hall on the main level. Music was often heard being played at the dance hall by groups such as George Bryant and his band, seen here. (Courtesy of the Great Plains Black History Museum in Omaha, Nebraska.)

Widely regarded as the top venue in North Omaha for jazz and blues music, the Dreamland Ballroom helped to fill a gap by providing a dancing spot for the Black community. For many years, Ak-sar-ben balls were segregated, resulting in the Dreamland Ballroom holding the Coronation Ball, which was modeled after the Ak-sar-ben event. The yearly occasion recognized leaders within the city's African American community, and the Beau Brummell Club (sometimes spelled Brummel), seen here, eventually became the sponsor of the event. (Image BF5795-001 from the Bostwick-Frohardt Collection, owned by KM3TV and on permanent loan to the Durham Museum, Omaha, Nebraska.)

With growing crowds and smart management, Dreamland Ballroom quickly became known as a frequent stop for top-name performers. Musical legends such as Duke Ellington, Louis Armstrong, Fats Domino, and Nat "King" Cole all played at the Dreamland Ballroom. Even the famed Ruth Brown (right) made an appearance at the facility. Performers who began in Nebraska proved just as popular, including the Preston Love Orchestra and the Dixie Ramblers. (From the Goin' to Kansas City Collection, courtesy of Jimmy Jewell and the Kansas City Museum in Kansas City, Missouri.)

During World War II, the military turned Dreamland Ballroom into a United Service Organizations (USO) Club for a short period of time. The club was specifically for African American troops in the city, as other facilities were segregated. Dances were still held at the ballroom during this period, including formal events put on for servicemen. After the conclusion of the war, owner Jimmy Jewell Jr. sued the government because of damage done to the building and reopened Dreamland Ballroom to the public. (From the Goin' to Kansas City Collection, courtesy of Jimmy Jewell and the Kansas City Museum in Kansas City, Missouri.)

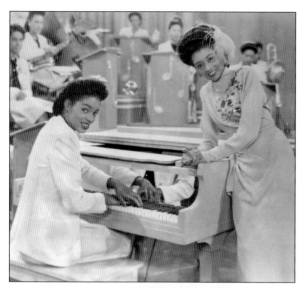

Postwar, the Dreamland Ballroom was once again a popular dance venue. Bands were recruited, including the International Sweethearts of Rhythm, a prominent group that featured Anna Mae Winburn (right). As a hub within its Omaha neighborhood, Dreamland continued to operate until 1965, when ownership closed the ballroom for good, echoing the fate of many such dance halls in Nebraska at the time. The Jewell Building is now listed in the National Register of Historic Places. (From the Goin' to Kansas City Collection, courtesy of Jimmy Jewell and the Kansas City Museum in Kansas City, Missouri.)

NAT TOWLES
and his Orchestra
Management
HOWARD WHITE
1506 Spring Street
OMAHA, NEBRASKA

The Carnation Ballroom, also known as the Carnation Lounge, was another popular dance hall in North Omaha. A 1954 advertisement in the *Omaha Star* highlighted an upcoming fundraiser dance at the Carnation Ballroom, which featured a "top-notch array of star-studded talent" consisting of eight different bands performing in one night, including the Nat Towles Orchestra, seen in the publicity photograph here. (From the Goin' to Kansas City Collection, courtesy of Jimmy Jewell and the Kansas City Museum in Kansas City, Missouri.)

The Roseland Dance Hall in Omaha was located on the second floor of this store building at Sixteenth and Douglas Streets. It was the site of an incident in 1930 involving excessive drinking and a young man shooting himself in the shoulder while the band was playing. The *Omaha World-Herald* reported that "a brief intermission was taken" while the gentleman was escorted to an ambulance and, from there, a hospital. He survived his injury, and the rest of the dance hall patrons called for an encore from the band, bringing the dance back into full swing. (Image BF2332-007 from the Bostwick-Frohardt Collection, owned by KM3TV and on permanent loan to the Durham Museum, Omaha, Nebraska.)

Omaha's Fort Omaha was also the site of dances, like the truck drivers' dance shown here. The 1918 event attracted a large crowd to the decorated hall. The *Omaha Daily News* reported that it was often military officers or an association of officers in charge of planning dance events, such as the monthly dances held at Fort Omaha as early as 1909. (Image BF4-179 from the Bostwick-Frohardt Collection, owned by KM3TV and on permanent loan to the Durham Museum, Omaha, Nebraska.)

The Chermot Ballroom in Omaha opened in 1931. The location immediately gained popularity among the local citizens, with famous performers providing music for dances on many occasions. Although some of them played at the Chermot before they made it big, Omaha's size did make it possible to book such acts as Frank Sinatra, Tommy Dorsey, Benny Goodman, Duke Ellington, Louis Armstrong, Guy Lombardo, and Lawrence Welk throughout its run. (Image BF4680-003 from the Bostwick-Frohardt Collection, owned by KM3TV on permanent loan to the Durham Museum, Omaha, Nebraska.)

When the Chermot Ballroom first opened, it was reported in the *Omaha Evening Bee-News* that "several hundred persons" were turned away from its first dance due to the venue reaching its capacity. Many dance halls throughout the state had managers or other staff to monitor dancers and throw out anyone who was becoming unruly or problematic in order to provide a better experience for other attendees. (Image JS18A-354 from the John S. Savage Collection, from the Durham Museum, Omaha, Nebraska. Copyright held by the *Omaha World-Herald*, Omaha, Nebraska.)

Omaha's Chermot Ballroom had a capacity of over 1,000 people, and the dance hall proved to be a well-liked location for high school dances and private events. In an *Omaha World-Herald* interview, a 1940 graduate recalled that they were able to "hire a 10-piece orchestra and a singer, under union contract, to play three hours for only $69." These relatively low prices made ballroom dances accessible to most youth, and the activity was a popular one. (Image JS18A-356 from the John S. Savage Collection, from the Durham Museum, Omaha, Nebraska. Copyright held by the *Omaha World-Herald*, Omaha, Nebraska.)

Omaha's Chermot Ballroom had been open for just over a decade when a fire caused extensive damage to the building in 1943. Here, cleanup efforts are underway amid the rubble. The fire took place only a few short hours after a dance was held there. Ownership rebuilt the ballroom and reopened afterward; however, another blaze in 1947 ended the Chermot Ballroom's presence in Omaha for good. The location has since been the site of business developments. (Image JS22A[4]-213 from the John S. Savage Collection, from the Durham Museum, Omaha, Nebraska. Copyright held by the *Omaha World-Herald*, Omaha, Nebraska.)

The Kitty Clover Potato Chip Company at Twenty-Fourth and Pierce Streets in Omaha may not seem to have anything to do with dancing at first glance. However, the building was a dance hall prior to its ownership by the chip company. There are likely many other structures throughout Nebraska, still standing or now gone, that once hosted dancing without any indication of such remaining today. (Image BF5321-002 from the Bostwick-Frohardt Collection, owned by KM3TV on permanent loan to the Durham Museum, Omaha, Nebraska.)

At the intersection of Twenty-Fifth and Grant Streets in Omaha, an unidentified dance hall was destroyed by a devastating tornado that struck the town in 1913. While one of the most destructive weather events in Omaha's history, the tornado was only one occasion in which a natural disaster struck down a ballroom somewhere within Nebraska. Floods, fires, heavy snowfalls, extreme winds, and other conditions often spelled an untimely end for dance halls across the state. (Author's collection.)

Three

SOUTHEASTERN NEBRASKA

A large number of dance halls in the southeastern region of Nebraska were Bohemian facilities. While these buildings were primarily gathering places for fraternal organizations, they often doubled as dance halls. The Czech heritage of the settlers who built these facilities shaped their perception of dancing, resulting in a fondness of and appreciation for the being passed passing down from each generation to the next. Outside of the more rural communities in southeastern Nebraska, Lincoln stands out as a larger city, with more ballrooms and dance halls to underline its size. Though smaller than Omaha, Lincoln's dancing landscape also featured hotel ballrooms and massive stand-alone dance halls. Some of the facilities in the region included the Appleton Community Center in Appleton; Barneston Community Center and the ZCBJ Hall in Barneston; the Beatrice Club Rooms, the Beatrice Country Club, the Beatrice Elks Club, the Beatrice Opera House, Beatrice Senior High, Nichols' Hall, and the VFW Hall in Beatrice; the Bee Parish Hall, the MWA Hall, and the ZCBJ Dance Hall in Bee; the Brainard Fire Hall, the Dus Tavern, the KD Hall, and the Soukup and Petrzilka Tavern in Brainard; the Fireman's Hall, the Sokol Hall, Turners' Hall, and the ZCBJ Hall in Bruno; the American Legion Hall, the Blue River Lodge, Liberty Pavilion, St. James Hall, the Tuxedo Park Dance Hall, and the VFW Hall in Crete; the Armory, Bunting's Building, the David City Auditorium, and the Thorpe Opera House, briefly known as Etting's Opera House, in David City; the Catholic Workman Hall, the Dwight Parish Hall, Dwight Public School, the Legion Club, Smitty's Bar and Grill, and the ZCBJ Hall in Dwight; the Fairbury Elks Club Room in Fairbury; the Fairmont Dance Hall in Fairmont; the Crystal Beach Pavilion, the Falls City Armory, and the MWA Hall in Falls City; the CSPS Hall in Humboldt; Harry and Mary's and Patrick's in Jansen; the Masonic Temple in Lincoln; Grant Memorial Hall, the Student Activities Building, and the Student Union Ballroom, all at the university in Lincoln; the Loma Parish Hall in Loma; Rut's Pavilion in Milligan; Brown's Park and the Elks Building in Nebraska City; the Odell Community Center in Odell; the TJ Sokol Hall, later a ZCBJ Hall, in Plattsmouth; the Pleasant Hill Dance Hall in Pleasant Hill; Fujan's Hall and the Prague Opera House in Prague; the Rulo Catholic Church Hall in Rulo; the Seward School Auditorium in Seward; Eller's Hall, the Fizzletown Dance Hall, King's Ballroom, and the Shelby Hotel Dance Hall in Shelby; Turkey Creek Hall in Shickley; the Staplehurst Community Hall in Staplehurst; the Swanton Dance Hall in Swanton; the Elms Ballroom in Syracuse; the Table Rock Dance Hall in Table Rock; the ZCBJ Hall in Tobias; the Odd Fellows building and the Ulysses Dance Hall in Ulysses; the Utica Auditorium and the Utica Dance Hall in Utica; Community Hall in Valparaiso; Scott's Lake and the Wahoo Community Center in Wahoo; Parish Hall, the Ponderosa Bar, and Weston Hall in Weston; and Assembly Hall, the Elks Home, Stein's Dance Pavilion, the York Country Club, and York's Beach in York. Each of these dance halls, alongside those throughout this chapter, demonstrate the powerful connections that the rural communities of southeastern Nebraska shared with one another through dancing and cultural events.

Prague's National Hall was built by the National Hall Association, a conglomerate of local organizations, each of which had counterparts operating a dance hall independently elsewhere in the state. The group consisted of two ZCBJ lodges, the area Czech-Slavonian Workman Benevolent Association, the Prague Volunteer Fire Department, Prague's American Legion, the community Sokol group, and the local Modern Woodmen of America (MWA) chapter. The size of Prague necessitated the collaboration to fund and construct the hall. (Author's collection.)

Throughout its opening year in 1964, the Starlite Ballroom offered a dance on Halloween and Thanksgiving, among other dates. The dance hall is still standing today, four miles west of Wahoo. Although excessive winds and a fire damaged the ballroom upon different occasions, local investment has kept the facility in operation. (Author's collection.)

Wanahoo Park in Wahoo was the home of a popular dance pavilion for many decades. The venue had its origins with the investments of local businessmen after World War I had ended. A history of the pavilion at the Saunders County Historical Society recalls that work on the project involved the construction of "an island with a pavilion surrounded by a moat filled with water from nearby Sandy Creek." Johnson's Orchestra from Fremont provided music for the opening reception in October 1920. (Courtesy of the Saunders County Historical Society and Museum.)

In 1948, Wahoo's Wanahoo Park changed ownership, and the dance pavilion was renamed Dance Island. The Dance Island pavilion continued to host dances for over another decade, but repeated flooding damaged the dance floor of the facility. The Saunders County Historical Society's records show that following each flood, the floor would be "sanded down and refinished" so dancing could resume, but Dance Island itself would close in 1963. A 1967 fire destroyed the pavilion. (Courtesy of the Saunders County Historical Society and Museum.)

Although Brainard's ZCBJ Hall held a connection to the Czech fraternal organization, the facility was available for use by various local groups. The American Legion held a Prize Dance on Armistice Day in 1935, with "40 useful articles . . . to be given away for free." The *Brainard Clipper* marketed that the Pilsener Orchestra would provide music for the event. (Author's collection.)

States Ballroom in Bee is a unique building with a dome-shaped roof atop a 12-sided structure. Now listed in the National Register of Historic Places, the dance hall commonly hosted at least two dances throughout a week's time, one for the general public and one for a wedding reception. Advertisements often mentioned both events together. (Courtesy of the Nebraska State Historical Society Photograph Collections.)

The Seward Amusement Association Dance Pavilion was located on the property of a larger entertainment park, much like many other pavilions in Nebraska. With dozens of musician groups to select from each year, the *Seward County Independent* noted that a quickly rising "favorite of favorites" was the Dixie Ramblers. This African American band was brought in repeatedly and "proved to be the most popular of all available dance bands" for the venue. (Courtesy of the Nebraska State Historical Society Photograph Collections.)

The Flying V outside of Utica was a restaurant, ballroom, and airport—all in one facility. The *Omaha World-Herald* noted that, in its prime, the dance hall saw an average of 800 dancers each weekend that music was provided. The facility was operated by the Volzkes of Utica, and they told the *Lincoln Journal Star* in 1975 that, despite a no-jeans-allowed rule, they were "getting more of a young crowd" participating in dances, particularly when country bands performed. (Courtesy of Lonny Hansen of the Lonny Lynn Orchestra.)

Lincoln's Sangerfest Hall was one of the oldest recorded dance facilities in the state. As early as 1885, the *Lincoln Journal Star* announced a "4th of July hop" on-site, which was planned by "Fred Poschen, the builder." While dancing certainly was at its peak in the mid-1900s, the *Lincoln Nebraska State Journal* has references to a "grand ball" held at Sangerfest Hall, also in 1885, far before the height of dance halls' popularity. (Courtesy of the Nebraska State Historical Society Photograph Collections.)

The Scottish Rite Temple in Lincoln was used most often by clubs and societies within the state's capital. Groups such as the Lincoln chapter of DeMolay, the Society of Secretaries of Scottish Rite, and Job's Daughters would occupy the space for the elections of officers and new member initiations, usually with dances to follow the more formal activities. (Author's collection.)

At the Cornhusker Hotel in Lincoln, the local United Service Organizations (USO) held a dance for its members and their dates during the 1940s. The Cornhusker Hotel Ballroom was frequented by multiple organizations for dance events of this nature. Additionally, dance clubs would often host singles-only dances on Fridays throughout the 1970s, providing a way for community members to meet new people. (Courtesy of the Nebraska State Historical Society Photograph Collections.)

The Cornhusker Hotel Ballroom in Lincoln served a dual purpose for many groups. For example, the *Central High Register* noted that a 1949 high school journalism conference concluded with "a banquet and a dance," both in the hotel's ballroom. The ability to host the complementary functions in the same location benefitted the hotel greatly, attracting large group gatherings to the event space. (Courtesy of the Nebraska State Historical Society Photograph Collections.)

The Pla-Mor Ballroom in Lincoln featured numerous styles of dancing. A 1960 promotion in the *Lincoln Star* mentioned that "fox trots and waltzes [were] gaining popularity." These accessible public dances meant that many Nebraskans could take part in the social activities so long as they could cover the cost of admission at the door. Various bands provided tunes, including Ruth Coleman's All-Girl Orchestra, seen here. (Courtesy of the Nebraska State Historical Society Photograph Collections.)

Lincoln's Pla-Mor Ballroom has been one of the most popular and recognizable dance halls within the state. A 1951 advertisement in the *Lincoln Farm and Home News* for the iconic venue noted that people "must have ample recreation to stimulate [their] minds and make [them] fit for the coming of tomorrow, as well as interesting to [their] friends." Dancing at the Pla-Mor Ballroom was promoted as one of the best recreational activities available to achieve these standards. (Courtesy of the Nebraska State Historical Society Photograph Collections.)

Often hailed as a site of culture and social activity, the Pershing Memorial Auditorium in Lincoln was widely recognized for the iconic tile mural on the exterior of the building. Also a popular dance site, it held dances closer to the present day than many other dance halls. At a New Year's Eve dance in 1999, one attendee told reporters from the *Lincoln Journal Star* that she was "looking forward to another century of dancing." Despite this optimistic outlook, the Pershing Auditorium was torn down in 2023. (Author's collection.)

Lincoln's Airplane and Flying School sometimes held dances for groups of cadets, like the one shown here, featuring music by Leo J. Beck and his orchestra. While many smaller towns did not have specific ballrooms or dance halls and instead used community buildings, this was not the case in Lincoln. Instead, the celebration shown here is an example of a private event, which could take place in any facility large enough to hold dancers and musicians. Businesses and schools were only some of the places this occurred. (Courtesy of the Nebraska State Historical Society Photograph Collections.)

Even in the largest cities of Nebraska, facilities not specifically designated as ballrooms were used for dances. This Catholic Youth Organization dance in 1949 took place in a gymnasium in Lincoln, and the large floor proved to be a solid dance space. Despite the many dance halls available, sometimes it made more sense for groups to utilize nontraditional facilities, particularly for youth dances, as is common today. (Courtesy of the Nebraska State Historical Society Photograph Collections.)

King's Dance Hall in Lincoln was owned by the same family that built the King's Ballrooms in both Norfolk and Shelby. A part of the Capitol Beach Amusement Park, King's hosted numerous dances and parties, sometimes advertised in newspapers, such as the *Lincoln Nebraska State Journal*, to be held "every nite but Monday." Here, some Elgin Watch Company employees are enjoying an outing at King's. (Courtesy of the Nebraska State Historical Society Photograph Collections.)

The original governor's mansion in Lincoln contained a ballroom for formal functions. In 1922, the *Lincoln Nebraska State Journal* described that the ballroom was "decorated in gold and blue, complete with various flowers and an attractive lattice." The lower rooms of the mansion were "decorated in a Hawaiian effect" at the same dance, which was attended by 150 guests. (Author's collection.)

The Lincoln Chamber of Commerce offered dances at its facility quite often, keeping the organization involved within the community on the social scene as well as the economic. In 1942, a list of "recreation for soldiers" in the *Lincoln Journal Star* mentioned a dance at the chamber of commerce with the Lincolnettes on an upcoming Saturday night. (Courtesy of the Nebraska State Historical Society Photograph Collections.)

Turnpike Ballroom, located just south of Lincoln, was sometimes called the Turnpike Dance Hall or the Pike. As one of the largest and most recognizable dance halls in the state, it fulfilled a need within the area after the city's original auditorium was destroyed in a 1928 fire. Unfortunately, the Turnpike would eventually go up in flames like its auditorium predecessor, foreshadowing the decline of big ballroom dancing in the area. (Courtesy of the Nebraska State Historical Society Photograph Collections.)

The Turnpike Ballroom was often very busy, thanks in part to its location and the quality of bands it provided for the public. Former attendees recollected in a *Lincoln Journal Star* interview that "if you wanted to impress a girl," the Turnpike was the place to go, and that it was likely "many people met their future husbands and wives there." It was not unusual for the entire dance floor to be packed with couples. (Courtesy of the Nebraska State Historical Society Photograph Collections.)

The Turnpike Ballroom's bandstand was the stage for numerous icons of music during the time the facility was in operation. A *Lincoln Journal Star* article reviewing the hall's history listed such performers as Duke Ellington, Glenn Miller, Paul Whitman, Louis Armstrong, Lawrence Welk, Bob Hope, and Ella Fitzgerald, among dozens of others. (Courtesy of the Nebraska State Historical Society Photograph Collections.)

The original Turnpike Ballroom burned down in 1935, but ownership swiftly rebuilt, and by 1936, the dance hall was back in operation. However, a quarter of a century later, a blaze in early 1961 leveled the iconic structure once again. Coinciding with "the number of touring bands dwindling," management told the *Lincoln Journal Star* that the Turnpike's days of entertaining the masses were over. (Courtesy of the Nebraska State Historical Society Photograph Collections.)

Located within Antelope Park in Lincoln, the Auld Pavilion was also called the Antelope Dance Pavilion. This ninth-grade dance taking place in 1961 is one of many in a long line reaching well into the 21st century. While the frequency of activities at many such facilities has since declined, the *Lincoln Journal Star* reports that the pavilion still holds events, such as the Leo Lonnie Orchestra in 2010 and the Lincoln Irish Dancers in 2017. (Courtesy of the Nebraska State Historical Society Photograph Collections.)

Auld Pavilion held dances regularly for the citizens of Lincoln, although not everyone was always welcome. The *Lincoln Journal Star* reported in 1919 that the dance pavilion would be reserved for Lincoln's Black residents for one night. They had requested the pavilion for one night each week, but that had been dismissed as "improbable," with officials instead opting to occasionally allow the space to be specifically reserved. (Author's collection.)

The City Auditorium in York is a large, impressive building with a track record of drawing in equally large and impressive crowds for dances. In 1946, when Lawrence Welk provided music for a dance, the building was packed full of Nebraskans from as far out as Broken Bow as well as a few folks from Kansas. The 1,300-person audience was the result of efforts by the York Chamber of Commerce dance committee, which the *York Daily News-Times* commended for its dedication to bringing in "top flight talent." (Author's collection.)

The ZCBJ Lodge near Dorchester, more commonly known as Tabor Hall, was slightly nontraditional in many senses. Although most dance halls charged less for women, in an attempt to encourage them to attend either alone or alongside their partner, an advertisement from 1933 indicated that both men and women would be charged a quarter to dance. Another uncommon occasion at the hall was a play performance and dance held back-to-back on a Sunday, scheduled unusually late, with an 8:00 p.m. start time. The *Dorchester Star* predicted the dance would not begin until "after midnite," which was quite late for a dance to commence. (Courtesy of the Nebraska State Historical Society Photograph Collections.)

The Sokol Auditorium in Crete, as with many Sokol halls, served multiple purposes within the community. This original frame building from 1891 burned down in 1913, being replaced by the still-active brick auditorium found in downtown Crete today. The auditorium was the place to be for both local play productions and dances. These activities helped locals stay connected with one another, and they kept many people involved in helping with the events. Notices in the *Crete News* promoted performers for the venue, including Kolman's Harmony Boys in 1937 and Horovka's Orchestra in 1938. (Courtesy of the Nebraska State Historical Society Photograph Collections.)

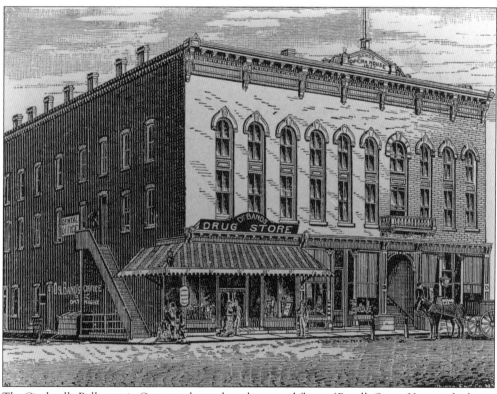

The Cinderella Ballroom in Crete was located on the second floor of Band's Opera House, which was built in 1877. The second floor was renovated in 1929 to operate as a dance space, but the venture was short-lived, as the approach of the Great Depression left the dance hall an unsuccessful business idea. Even so, those few years of operation left an impact upon the community, and the dances attracted large crowds. (Courtesy of the Nebraska State Historical Society Photograph Collections.)

The ZCBJ-associated Milligan Auditorium was a popular site, particularly throughout the 1930s and 1940s. In 1942, the *Milligan Review* reported that an upcoming dance at the auditorium would offer a variety of dances, including "Ladies' Choice, May Pole, and Everything!" There were often different types of dancing to be found within Nebraska, such as some that necessitated a caller to provide instructions for the next moves. (Author's collection.)

Located near Western, the Saline Center Lodge Hall was associated with the ZCBJ of Nebraska. The hall was constructed in 1939 and hosted numerous dances for residents of the surrounding rural communities. The *Western Wave* reported that a 1952 polio fundraiser dance raised $230.14 for the cause, with the rent of the facility being waived as a donation. The structure is now listed in the National Register of Historic Places. (Author's collection.)

The Country Club Park Pavilion in Wilber was prepared for the wild Nebraska weather conditions at any time. When cold temperatures arrived, canvas material was used to cover the shelter to keep the band and dancers inside warm. Although many advertisements for the pavilion stated it was free to dance, there was often a gate fee to enter the park where the pavilion stood. (Courtesy of the Nebraska State Historical Society Photograph Collections.)

While it is now an abandoned structure on a gravel county road, Brush Creek Hall near Wilber once offered the promise of a "newly waxed floor [and] music by Savages Orchestra" in the *Wilber Republican*. The Circling Square Club held regular dances at Brush Creek Hall. Club members once sang happy birthday for a three year old at the hall, and the occasion even made the local newspaper. (Author's collection.)

Notably the Czech capital of the United States, Wilber had several active dance halls for many years, including its Sokol Auditorium, also called the Sokol Pavilion. Still standing in downtown Wilber today, the building was used as a performing arts center for the local Sokol Players' Guild as well as for dances. On Christmas Day 1931, a lively dance immediately followed a Sokol play production, keeping the community members together at the auditorium for the holiday. (Courtesy of the Nebraska State Historical Society Photograph Collections.)

The Beatrice Auditorium was the site of multiple community dances throughout the years, but a 1974 junior-senior prom demonstrated the declining popularity of such events in later years. It was apparent at the *Wizard of Oz*–themed prom that there was a 50 percent decline in students' attendance, and those who did attend wore more informal garb than in years prior. (Author's collection.)

The ZCBJ Hall northwest of Du Bois was dedicated in 1921. Since then, it has been the site of dances with music by Rudy Hubka's Orchestra, the Table Rock Orchestra, and Lad Tracek's Orchestra. The hall is an important piece of cultural heritage for the region and is now listed in the National Register of Historic Places. (Courtesy of the Nebraska State Historical Society Photograph Collections.)

The Prichard Auditorium in Falls City was constructed as part of the Works Progress Administration program in the 1930s. The building was funded in part by a memorial gift from Laura Prichard in honor of her husband, Leander, as well as other donors from the community who matched her total. In 1947, over a decade later, the Johnnie Cox Orchestra performed at the auditorium, proof that the community's passion for dancing and the facility was still strong. (Author's collection.)

Four

CENTRAL NEBRASKA

The dance halls in central Nebraska were found in clusters throughout the region, usually in areas of denser population. Each of the tri-city communities had a diverse array of ballrooms to offer their citizens. Moving northward, halls built by those with Danish heritage in the Dannebrog area provided more of a cultural impact, not unlike the German-influenced Liederkranz Auditorium in Grand Island. Some of the dance halls that could be found in central Nebraska include the Fairgrounds Pavilion and the Opera House in Albion; Union Hall in Aurora; the Blue Hill Legion Ballroom and the Blue Hill Opera House in Blue Hill; the Butte Legion Ballroom in Butte; the 4-H Building at the Merrick County Fairgrounds, the American Legion Club, the Central City Opera House, City Hall, Dodson Barn, Harmony Hall, Liberty Hall, Rose Wilde Hall, and the Warm Slough Schoolhouse in Central City; Campbell's Hall in Clarks; the Clay Center Round Barn near Clay Center; the Palace Theater in Clearwater; the Ancient Order of United Workmen (AOUW) Hall and Malick's Park in Cowles; Park Hall in Dannebrog; the Doniphan Opera House and town hall in Doniphan; the Summerland Dance Pavilion in Ewing; Dobry Pavilion and the ZCBJ Hall in Farwell; Moon's Dance Hall, the Odd Fellows Hall, Spelts Opera House, the VFW Hall, and Wilson's Hall in Fullerton; the Gibbon Opera House in Gibbon; the Giltner Opera House in Giltner; Cherry Street Hall, Dreamland Dance Hall, and the Islanda Ballroom in Grand Island; the Youth Center in Greeley; the Guide Rock Legion Hall and the Guide Rock Opera House in Guide Rock; the American Legion Hall, Brandes Hall, the Eagles Club Hall, the Hastings Young Men's Christian Association (YMCA), the KHAS auditorium, and Spanish Village in Hastings; Havens Dance Hall in Havens; the Buffalo County Improvement Hall Club, Dickie Dugan's Dance Hall, the Kearney Armory, the Kearney Elks Lodge, including the Circle Lounge, and the Lake Kearney Pavilion in Kearney; Wichman's Dance Pavilion in Loup City; the IOOF Hall and the Lynch Ballroom in Lynch; the Minden Opera House in Minden; Legion Hall in North Loup; Nysted Hall in Nysted; the American Legion Ballroom, Danceland, the Knights of Columbus Hall, and Oak View Park Dance Pavilion in O'Neill; Andy's Dance Hall in Poole; the Antelope Valley Grange Hall, Finder's Hall, the Prairie Creek Dance Hall, and Yanda's Pavilion in Ravenna; the Besse Auditorium and Veterans Hall in Red Cloud; Pioneer Ballroom, the Saladin Opera House, and Wooster's Barn in Silver Creek; the ZCBJ Hall in Spencer; the Knights of Columbus Hall and the ZCBJ Hall in St. Paul; George Wallinger's barn and the Stuart Auditorium in Stuart; and the Upland Auditorium in Upland. Each of these locations as well as those examined within this chapter provided people with somewhere to socialize and dance together.

Located outside of Central City along the Platte River, Riverside Park Pavilion is now listed in the National Register of Historic Places. When the updated pavilion was opened in the summer of 1940, it was reported in the *Central City Republican-Nonpareil* that "one thousand people from over twenty-five Nebraska counties and from seven other states" attended the occasion. At the time, it was considered by many to be both the biggest and best dance floor west of Omaha. (Author's collection.)

The City Auditorium in Spalding proved to be quite the popular venue when it hosted a "triple wedding dance" on April 15, 1947, for three area couples. The Molt-Wheeler, Estey-Seamann, and Dickey-Seamann weddings occurred within three days of one another—the Seamann brothers were both married on the same day—so the dances were held at the auditorium together, making for a massive community celebration that made the *Spalding Enterprise* newspaper. (Author's collection.)

The Aurora Opera House in Aurora was a dance site very early on in the community's history. In 1885, the *Republican-Register* reminded readers about the upcoming "Thanksgiving ball at the Opera House," and in 1886, the paper covered the opera house's "Grand Masquerade Ball." A year later, in 1887, the *Aurora News-Register* advertised a "Grand Holiday Dance at the opera house," which everyone in town was invited to. (Courtesy of the Hamilton County Historical Society/Plainsman Museum of Aurora, Nebraska.)

Aurora's iconic Temple Craft Hall was active even before the 1900s. The *Republican-Register* reported in 1899 that the hall held "the first of a series of three dances," given by a "crowd of young people." The event was well attended, demonstrating that the generation of youth at the time was happily invested in dancing as leisure. The evening concluded with the "Home, Sweet Home waltz." (Courtesy of the Hamilton County Historical Society/ Plainsman Museum of Aurora, Nebraska.)

The Platt-Deutsche Hall in Grand Island contained a ballroom on the second floor. The grand event space sometimes required attendees to wear less grand apparel to participate in the fun, such as when "an overall and apron dance" was held there. Management of the dance hall was insistent that everyone was "to appear properly attired" for the occasion and made such demands clear in the *Grand Island Daily Independent*. (Courtesy of the Stuhr Museum of the Prairie Pioneer.)

Grand Island's Platt-Deutsche Hall was used for specific dancing events as well. In 1944, when Mr. and Mrs. Carl F. Stoltenberg celebrated their 50th wedding anniversary with a dance, it was held at the hall. The *Grand Island Daily Independent* noted that Carl had been the "janitor of the Platt Deutsche Hall" for a decade prior to retirement, meaning the location of the golden anniversary celebration held special significance for the two 70-year-olds. (Courtesy of the Stuhr Museum of the Prairie Pioneer.)

Schimmer's Lake near Grand Island was an amusement park that offered dances to the public. In 1935, the *Grand Island Herald* announced dances for three nights in a row over Labor Day weekend. Another promotion for the facility in the *Grand Island Daily Independent* boasted that Schimmer's Lake was home to "the largest dance hall in the state." (Courtesy of the Stuhr Museum of the Prairie Pioneer.)

Grand Island's Schimmer's Lake Dance Hall was also known as the Sand Krog Tavern. The *Grand Island Daily Independent* reported that the dual "bar and dance hall . . . was a popular gathering place for many years." In 1906, the space was too tiny to continue holding dances, so a pavilion was built on the property. After heavy snowfall collapsed the roof of the pavilion in 1932, a new one was constructed in 1933. (Courtesy of the Stuhr Museum of the Prairie Pioneer.)

Construction on the Liederkranz Auditorium in Grand Island began in 1911 and was completed in 1912. Constructed for the local Liederkranz group, a German singing ensemble, the building was also utilized for various dances and, in later years, community events. Still standing today, the structure is listed in the National Register of Historic Places. (Author's collection.)

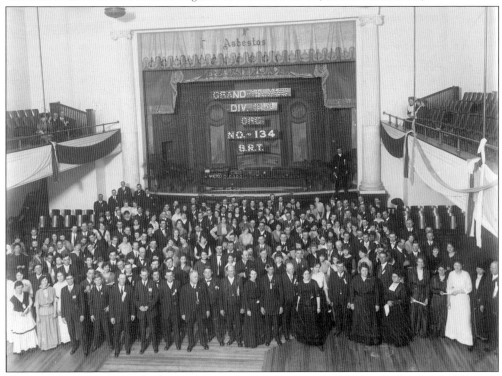

The Liederkranz hosted multiple United Service Organizations (USO) dances during World War II when an air base was established near Grand Island. Soldiers would attend the parties, and the *Grand Island Daily Independent* reported "copious quantities of hot dogs" being served by volunteers to the attendees at one of the larger dances in 1944. (Courtesy of the Stuhr Museum of the Prairie Pioneer.)

Grand Island's Liederkranz Auditorium was also the location of theatrical performances for the community. In 1936, the *Grand Island Daily Independent* publicized a "musical comedy with [the] Beck-Jungbluth 13-piece orchestra" providing the melodies. The same promotion added that the orchestra would also play for a dance at the Liederkranz following the show, making for a busy night for the musical group from Lincoln. (Courtesy of the Stuhr Museum of the Prairie Pioneer.)

The Glovera Ballroom in Grand Island often packed its weekend schedules with bands and performers, drawing in crowds for three nights in a row. When "Ada Leonard and her 16-piece girl band" played at the ballroom in 1942, the *Grand Island Daily Independent* dubbed it a "special big dance." The all-woman band stopped in Grand Island following a longer contract in Denver. The Glovera Ballroom burned down in 1954. (Courtesy of the Stuhr Museum of the Prairie Pioneer.)

Much like other hotels in more populated areas of the state, the Yancey Hotel in Grand Island offered its ballroom for use by the community as another source of both advertising and income. A series of evening dances hosted by the Young Married People's Dance Club took place within the hotel's ballroom. (Courtesy of the Stuhr Museum of the Prairie Pioneer.)

Throughout the early 1900s in particular, the Ancient Order of United Workmen (AOUW) Hall in Grand Island served as an exceptional dance hall for the community. In 1908, the *Grand Island Daily Independent* reported that a recent dance at the hall "was a success in every respect," resulting in another dance being scheduled for the next week. The AOUW Hall was the location of a "regular Saturday night dance" in 1916, demonstrating the popularity of the activity at the time. (Courtesy of the Stuhr Museum of the Prairie Pioneer.)

F.F. Suehlson's barn in Grand Island was often the host site for local dances in the early 1900s. The barn dance pictured here was held in 1905. Many rural towns would utilize barns for dancing if a hall was not readily available. The barns had enough space to accommodate dancers, making the practice common statewide. This tradition has held true into the present day, as barn dances are still popular in some communities. (Courtesy of the Stuhr Museum of the Prairie Pioneer.)

Grand Island's Elks Home was a busy facility, with a multitude of activities taking place within the building's walls. Particularly, the Elks Club hosted frequent dances and entertainment events for its membership. The *Grand Island Independent* noted in 1923 that "all Elks and their families" were welcome to enjoy a matinee dance at the home. (Author's collection.)

The St. Paul American Legion served as a dance hall for many years. Notably, in 1939, the *Phonograph* reported on the "annual American Legion Cow Dance," with an orchestra providing music for the occasion. The notice highlighted that the raised funds would go toward paying off the building, and that "besides having a good time and maybe getting a cow or some of the turkeys, geese, etc. that night," attendees would be supporting a "good cause." (Author's collection.)

Pleasure Isle Pavilion in Dannebrog was located on just the other side of a creek near town, meaning dancers crossed a bridge to get to the facility. The dance hall was impressive, with a large dance floor for attendees, a stage platform for the musicians, and equipment to control the temperature inside, meaning dances could be held any time of the year. (Courtesy of Columbia Hall.)

Columbia Hall in Dannebrog was constructed in 1908 by the local chapter of the Danish Brotherhood in America organization. The facility was used as a meeting place for the group, which was large due to the concentrated Danish settlement in Dannebrog, but the second floor was often utilized for community dances. The building, seen on the far right, is now listed in the National Register of Historic Places. (Courtesy of Columbia Hall.)

Dannebrog's Columbia Hall was the site of some interesting events in 1941. While a dance for soldiers who had been drafted for the war effort was taking place on-site, an explosion occurred in the building. The *Dannebrog News* reported that it was "believed to be a time bomb," and that part of the hall had been damaged. While nobody was hurt, a Federal Bureau of Investigation (FBI) agent, shown here, was sent to examine the scene, but nothing came of the incident. (Courtesy of Columbia Hall.)

The Winter Garden Ballroom in Hastings was operated by Mr. and Mrs. Lib Phillips for a 15-year tenure from 1921 to 1936. The gorgeous facility hosted music from the likes of Jacque Winroth and Tommy Morgan. The dance hall was often used to help fundraise for local organizations, such as the Lady Bowlers, whose dance benefit cost only a dime for admission. (Courtesy of the Adams County Historical Society.)

The Hastings City Auditorium was built in 1924. The facility is notable for its wide usage by local groups for different dance celebrations. In 1932, the *Hastings Daily Tribune* documented the "attendance of approximately three hundred" people at St. Margaret's Guild Thanksgiving Dance, a yearly event for the community. Eddie Jungbluth's 13-piece orchestra out of Lincoln played at the affair, and the dance was recognized as "one of the most important events of the fall season in Hastings" by the paper. (Author's collection.)

Although not the only place to dance in town, the Hastings Masonic Temple maintained a popular following with recurring events, such as its "back to school dance." The *Morning Spotlight* described the 1936 rendition of the dance favorably, as it featured the lively Jack Russell and his orchestra, and was well decorated, with "blackboards with school slogans" on them placed throughout the room. (Author's collection.)

The Lib's Park Pavilion in Hastings sometimes held dances sponsored by the Hastings Boosters. In 1941, the *Hastings Daily Tribune* boasted that one such dance highlighted music by "Art Kassel and His Kassels in the Air . . . featuring Cub. Higgins, the one-man band within the band." The pavilion was known to bring in the "most popular dance bands" from different regions of the country for season opening shows. (Courtesy of the Adams County Historical Society.)

The Municipal Auditorium in Kenesaw offered a "large and spacious floor of over 9,000 square feet of dance space" for the community to enjoy. In 1934, a Municipal Auditorium benefit dance was held to break in the new flooring, with the popular nine-piece Adolph Seminek orchestra, a crowd favorite from Lincoln's Capitol Beach Park, scheduled to play. The *Kenesaw Progress* reported that "dancers [from] miles around" attended the event. (Courtesy of the Nebraska State Historical Society Photograph Collections.)

The 1733 Ranch Dance Hall near Kearney, also known as the 1733 Park Ballroom, was notable for being located on the site of a ranch that was 1,733 miles from both Boston and San Francisco. Formerly a large barn, the facility could accommodate around 1,000 people. The dance hall collapsed in 1964, leaving the formerly prominent structure in ruins. (Image from Pictorial Kearney, Nebraska Greetings, courtesy of the Buffalo County Historical Society/Trails & Rails Museum.)

In its earliest days, the Kearney Opera House was known as the Model Opera House, and the styles of dancing that took place there varied widely. A 1938 *Kearney Hub* article reflected back upon these dances, including the "old fashioned waltz, the schottische, polka, and the square dances, which included quadrilles, lancers, Virginia reel, Cecillian circle, Dan Tucker, the Money Musk, and a sort of combination polka and schottische." (Courtesy of the Buffalo County Historical Society/Trails & Rails Museum.)

The Kearney Opera House in Kearney had a long history of dancing and entertainment. As early as 1892, the *Kearney Hub* covered a "fine dancing party" with "about fifty couples present" at the opera house. The fifth floor of the building was utilized for the occasion, and music was played by the Midway Orchestra for all to enjoy. (Author's collection.)

The Fort Kearney Hotel's Crystal Ballroom was often the site of dinner dances for community organizations. After the banquet was complete, attendees would dance to music provided by either local or regional bands, such as Ellis Frazier's Orchestra, the Club Commodore, Guy Hite's Orchestra, and Laddie Lysinger's Orchestra, among many others. (Author's collection.)

The Crystal Ballroom in the Fort Kearney Hotel in Kearney proved to be a valuable venue for the students living in town. Multiple groups from the college campus, including the Juanita and Sigma Theta Phi sororities, hosted formal dances in the ballroom, which were often themed with the calendar's upcoming holidays, such as Christmas or St. Patrick's Day. (Courtesy of the Buffalo County Historical Society/Trails & Rails Museum.)

Five

WESTERN NEBRASKA

Dance halls in western Nebraska were spread out and often entertained entire counties worth of people. The ballrooms here were crucial components within their respective communities—from both an economic and a recreational perspective. Some dance halls throughout western Nebraska and the panhandle include the Ainsworth Auditorium, the Crystal Ballroom, the JK Roller Rink, the Rex Bailey Dance Hall, and the Starlit Club in Ainsworth; the Dutch Mill, Grandview School, and Westside Hall in Alliance; Mary's Hall in Anselmo; the Ansley Legion Club, Elmer Hall, and the Odd Fellows Hall in Ansley; the high school auditorium, Legion Hall, and the Owl's Roost in Arcadia; Legion Hall, Myers' Dance Hall, and the Red, White, and Blue Hall in Arnold; the Knights of Columbus Hall and Memorial Hall in Atkinson; Dundy County Fairgrounds Quonset Building in Benkelman; the Jonson barn in Berwyn; the Brandon Community Hall in Brandon; Bernard's Pavilion, the Elks Hall, Moore's Roof Garden, and the Odd Fellows Hall in Broken Bow; Jonson's near Broken Bow; the Burwell Legion Hall in Burwell; Bryner's Hall in Callaway; the Campus Center Ballroom and the Chadron Student Center Ballroom, both at Chadron State College, and the Pace Ballroom in Chadron; the White Elephant Saloon in Cody; Woodman Hall in Comstock; the City Park Pavilion in Crawford; the Elsie Legion Hall and the Odd Fellows Hall in Elsie; Elyria Hall in Elyria; the Glen Dance Hall in Glen; Calling's Hall, the Gothenburg Opera House, and the Legion Hall in Gothenburg; the AOUW Hall, Crescent Ballroom, Kowalski Dance Studio, Perkins County Fairgrounds Dance Pavilion, and a schoolhouse in Grant; the Shady Beach Dance Pavilion, later called the Midway Dance Hall, between Grant and Ogallala; the Rainbow Ballroom in Halsey; the IOOF Hall and the Rocky Top Dance Hall in Harrison; the Chicken Roost Dance Hall and Reno's Dance Hall in Hay Springs; the ZCBJ Bohemian Dance Hall near Hemingford; the Amusement Park Dance Pavilion and the Holdrege Opera House in Holdrege; the Holstein Dance Hall in Holstein; the Quonset building in the Hull Community; Spady's Quonset in Imperial; Fraternal Hall and the Kimball Country Club in Kimball; the Lexington Armory and the Smith Opera House in Lexington; the American Legion Hall in Lisco; Lyman Hall in Lyman; the Madrid Legion Hall and Shafer's Building in Madrid; the Community Building and the Fire Hall in Mason City; the American Legion, the Armory Hall, the Carter Dance Hall, Diamond Hall, the Eagles Club, the Elks Club, Felling Field, Fleischmann Park, now Elks Park, Garden Dance Hall, the Gayway Ballroom-Cafe, the Keystone Hotel, Menard Opera House, Pastime Park, Ravenswood Pavilion, Rutt Hall, Uerling's Hall, and the YMCA in McCook; the Meadville Pavilion in Meadville; the Legion Hall in Merna; Milburn Hall in Milburn; Helm's Hall in Mitchell; the American Legion Hall in Morrill; Japanese Hall and the Knights of Columbus Hall in North Platte; Mary's Hall in Oconto; the Crystal Ballroom, Crystal Pavilion, the Elks Building, and the VFW Hall in Ogallala; the Masonic Hall and National Hall in Ord; the Palace Dance Hall and Priel's Opera House in Overton; the Dixie Belle Dance Hall in Oxford; the Lost Park Dance Pavilion and Valleyview Hall in Riverview; the Hosek Pavilion in Sargent; Danceland, the Elks Lodge, Gene's Dance Pavilion, Klub Ko Kay (later known as the Stomp Inn or the Beachcomer), the Scottsbluff National Guard Armory, the Stable Café, the VFW Hall, and Warrick's Dance Hall in Scottsbluff; Hale's Hall in Seneca; the Elks Lodge auditorium and Kreuger's Lake in Sidney; the Logan County Fairgrounds near Stapleton; the Legion Community Hall in Sutherland; the Grady Dance Hall in Valentine; the Venango Legion Hall in Venango; Wauneta High School Auditorium and Gym in Wauneta; and Westerville Dance Hall in Westerville. All of these dance halls helped to cultivate community throughout western Nebraska.

Located on the Keya Paha County Fairgrounds, the Norden Dance Pavilion has long been the site of dances, both during the county fair and throughout the rest of the summer. As early as 1931, the *Springview Herald* had an advertisement by the fair committee for a dance with "music by Bronson's Bostonians." The pavilion is now a Nebraska State Historic Site. (Author's collection.)

For a number of years, the American Legion Hall in Ainsworth hosted dances for high school students within the community. In 1943, staff from the nearby air base began utilizing the space for their own recreational purposes, resulting in a community effort to address the lack of a venue for youth dances. The crisis was averted when the board of education permitted dances to be held at the school auditorium. (Author's collection.)

Long Pine's Hidden Paradise dance pavilion was a grand structure with the capability to operate into the cooler months. The *Long Pine Journal* reported in 1919 that the "pavilion [had] been enclosed for the fall," enabling dancers to attend and dance until the much colder winter temperatures hit the area. (Courtesy of the Nebraska State Historical Society Photograph Collections.)

Hidden Paradise in Long Pine was one of the many dance halls in Nebraska to bring in popular orchestras made up of only women performers to provide music for community dances. Some of these orchestras included Maxine Cotton and her orchestra as well as the Cotterill Sisters Orchestra, pictured here. (Courtesy of the Nebraska State Historical Society Photograph Collections.)

Recognizable for its distinct architectural style, the Dunning Community Hall in Dunning was finished in 1938. It was built with support from the Works Progress Administration. The *Blaine County Booster*, a local newspaper that was frequently in opposition to Pres. Franklin D. Roosevelt and his policies, ceased coverage of the construction once funds were secured from Washington, DC, but later advertised dances and other events at the completed community center. (Author's collection.)

The Anselmo Community Hall was the site of American Legion dances for the surrounding area in the 1930s. A snippet of the *Anselmo Enterprise* in 1925, however, tells of a disappointing turnout for a dance at the Anselmo Community Hall. Lack of proper advertising for the event, paired with "everyone being so busy," were the attributed causes of the small public showing. (Author's collection.)

Oscar's Palladium in Sargent was named after Oscar Melham, who owned the facility and turned it into a popular dance hall from the 1940s through the 1970s. In a *Kearney Hub* interview, the present owners of the building recollected the height of dancing at the Palladium when kids, tired from the evening's activity, "piled coats on the floor in the corner and fell asleep" while their parents continued to dance the night away. (Courtesy of the Nebraska State Historical Society Photograph Collections.)

The Freeman Opera House in Sargent often held dances featuring the Sargent Band. In 1919, one dance was held to assist in the purchase of band uniforms; however, the cost of materials was so high at the time that they only made enough money to buy two outfits. The *Sargent Leader* found that the dance was well attended, and the band provided "each returned [World War I] soldier who attended a ticket free of charge." (Courtesy of the Nebraska State Historical Society Photograph Collections.)

Located at the intersection of two county roads near Comstock, the ZCBJ Hall, usually referred to as National Hall, held numerous events, including dances, for which those celebrating "birthdays and wedding anniversaries" were charged no admission fee. One listing of upcoming dances in the *Comstock News* noted that a dance at National Hall on November 21, 1959, would be the "last dance before Advent" that year. (Author's collection.)

Jungman Hall in rural Eureka township was initially built prior to 1923, being replaced at that time when the original structure burned down. The hall, which held dances, was affiliated with the local ZCBJ lodge and named for Josef Jungman, a Czech linguist. In 1969, the *Ord Quiz* published an article commemorating the hall's history, including the extensive construction of the facility, which required "hundreds of wagons pulled by two and four-horse teams to haul the building materials from Burwell and Comstock." (Courtesy of the Nebraska State Historical Society Photograph Collections.)

The Bohemian Hall in Ord was built by Czech settlers in the area, and it often served as a dance hall for all those in town. A 1936 announcement in the *Ord Quiz* advertised one such occasion at the Bohemian Hall when the Taylor Dance Club Orchestra was scheduled to play. The promotion, which was for an "Old-Time Community Dance," noted that admission for ladies was 10¢ and for men, 15¢. (Courtesy of the Nebraska State Historical Society Photograph Collections.)

One of many dance halls with the same name within Nebraska, the Dreamland Ballroom of Broken Bow was often filled with dancers. The structure was originally located in New Helena but was split into four sections and moved to Broken Bow in 1948. The *Custer County Chief* announced that the Custer County Fair offered a dance at Dreamland for four nights in a row in 1949, and the sale of the building two years later to the local Elks Lodge brought even more traffic to the ballroom for club meetings and dances. (Courtesy of the Custer County Historical Society.)

C. H. F. Steinmeier, Druggist, Ainsley, Nebr.

Woodman Hall in Ansley, misspelled on this postcard, often hosted to popular community dinner dances, much like its counterpart facilities in larger Nebraska cities. In 1900, an advertisement in the *Argosy and the Chronicle-Citizen* noted that following the conclusion of the meal, "[a]ll who can't dance, don't want to dance, or are to [sic] cranky to see others dance, [would] be allowed to retire" before the second half of the evening's activities began. The hall was operated by the local Modern Woodmen of America (MWA) group and was also called the Modern Woodmen Hall. It was later referred to as simply the Ansley Community Center. (Courtesy of the Custer County Historical Society.)

Hotel Dale in Holdrege contained a banquet hall, which was frequently the site of the local supper club's dances. In 1939, the *Holdrege Daily Citizen* reported that local high school students had hosted out-of-town guests "from Curtis, Oxford, and Orleans high schools" at a dance at Hotel Dale, with tunes provided "by radio orchestras." (Author's collection.)

In Holdrege's Municipal Auditorium, many famous bands from throughout the region performed. Often, these big name musicians had landed long-term contracts in states farther west but were recruited by Holdrege locals to furnish music for a dance in the small town while traveling through. This was the case for an orchestra known as The Nebraskans, who, having landed a summer-long gig in Estes Park, agreed to stop in Holdrege on the way to Colorado. (Author's collection.)

The cost of admission to a dance frequently varied depending upon the purpose of the event and the host organization. Another factor could be world events, reflected by an additional tax added to the price to get into a 1921 Thanksgiving dance at the Holdrege Municipal Auditorium due to the war. (Courtesy of the Don O. Lindgren Genealogy Library at the Nebraska Prairie Museum of Holdrege, Nebraska.)

The Alma City Auditorium and Sale Barn in Alma is presently listed in the National Register of Historic Places. The community building hosted numerous social events, including a special "show and dance" in 1933 featuring the Ray Bash Players. The occasion was promoted in the *Harlan County Journal* as a "two for one," with the show beginning at 8:15 p.m., followed by the dance at 10:00 p.m. (Author's collection.)

The Beaver City Auditorium held many events for the surrounding residents. Movies were shown, dances were hosted, and community meals were enjoyed at the facility. In 1922, the *Times-Tribune* promoted the orchestra that would perform at an upcoming dance featuring a variety of music. The instruments present included a "violin, mandola, cornet, piano, and drums," promising a fun time for all. (Author's collection.)

Locals often hosted balls or other dances at the Arapahoe Opera House. The *Public Mirror* advertised a 1912 Easter Ball, at which it would cost $1 to dance and 25¢ to spectate. When promoting an upcoming "band dance" at the opera house, the *Public Mirror* noted that the "band need[ed] the money," asking locals to come out, have a good time, and support the musical ensemble. (Author's collection.)

The Memorial Auditorium in McCook has served as a community space since its completion in 1939. The *McCook Republican* covered the opening event in the finished structure, appropriately an Armistice Day service, which was followed by the "first public entertainment" in the new building, a dance put on by local veterans organizations. (Author's collection.)

Located six miles north of Lexington in Dawson County, the Community House was a structure utilized for dances for many years. Beyond square dancing and modern dancing, the building also hosted a masquerade dance and other activities directed toward a younger demographic. Weekly dances throughout the course of the year, even in the winter months, were listed in the *Lexington Clipper-Herald* and kept the area's residents connected. (Courtesy of the Dawson County Historical Society.)

The Community House was home to the Rusty Gate Square Dance Club, which began around 1949. The club often recruited the youth of the surrounding communities to square dance together and meet one another. These regular activities at the dance hall were well attended, with the *Lexington Clipper and Dawson County Pioneer* boasting "usual attendance [of] 3 square or 24 people." (Courtesy of the Dawson County Historical Society.)

One of the earliest records of dancing in the state took place in Plum Creek, modern-day Lexington, at Johnson's Hotel. The dance was in commemoration of the United States of America's centennial celebration in July 1876. This dance card would have been utilized by its carrier to keep track of dance partners throughout the course of the festivities. (Courtesy of the Dawson County Historical Society.)

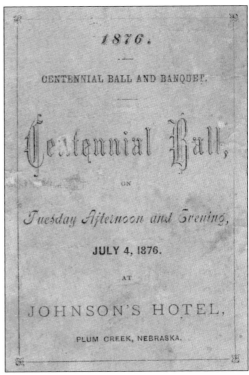

1876.

CENTENNIAL BALL AND BANQUET.

Centennial Ball,

ON

Tuesday Afternoon and Evening,

JULY 4, 1876.

AT

JOHNSON'S HOTEL,

PLUM CREEK, NEBRASKA.

As early as 1906, the year the building's construction was completed, Allen's Opera House in Cozad hosted dances or balls for those living in the area. A later advertisement in the *Cozad Local* for a Valentine's dance at the opera house stated that both "Good Music and a Good Time" were guaranteed. The structure is now listed in the National Register of Historic Places. (Courtesy of the Dawson County Historical Society.)

Dating as far back as the early 1900s, the Houston Hotel in Gothenburg provided space for dances in the Dawson County community. At a dance held in honor of Joe Schopp, many attendees "tripped the light fantastic," a common phrase at the time that referred to agile dancing. The *Gothenburg Independent* publicized another dance at the hotel for which "a couple of traveling men" played music for all the dancers present. (Courtesy of the Dawson County Historical Society.)

CO. HQS. SEP. 1957 N. PLATTE.

The Crystal Ballroom in North Platte, like many other ballrooms across Nebraska, would sometimes host fundraising events. In 1950, the *Telegraph-Bulletin* reported that a sorority held a "benefit dance . . . [for] the Special Service Room in the Lincoln School for Handicapped Children." Events of this nature showcase how ballrooms helped philanthropic and charitable efforts succeed throughout the state. (Courtesy of the Lincoln County Historical Society.)

North Platte's Crystal Ballroom was located inside of the Pawnee Hotel, and the facility welcomed many notable guests. In 1949, *The Tonight Show* host Johnny Carson (center) of Norfolk married Jody Wolcott (third from right) of North Platte, with a reception at the Crystal Ballroom. Pictured here are the newlyweds with others present at the party, including Johnny's brother and best man, Dick Carson (third from left). (Courtesy of the Lincoln County Historical Society.)

On Christmas Day 1939, the Crystal Ballroom held a dance that was attended by around 200 people, decorated for the occasion, and dubbed by the *North Platte Telegraph* as "one of the largest social functions of the year." Many couples hosted guests for a meal prior to the event, with some of them eating in the Pawnee Hotel itself before walking through the connected entrance of the ballroom, shown here, to the dance. (Courtesy of the Lincoln County Historical Society.)

North Platte's Jeffers Pavilion often promoted itself in local newspapers such as the *Telegraph-Bulletin* and the *Daily Bulletin* as "the dance spot of the Midwest" or at least "the hottest spot in town." The dance pavilion occasionally held a "free nite" during which there was "free admission for the first 10 couples" and "free dancing for everybody from 9:30 'till 10:00." (Courtesy of the Lincoln County Historical Society.)

Jeffers Pavilion hosted Lloyd Hunter and his orchestra in 1941 for a dance where the cost of admission was of particular interest to the community. It was noted in the *Lincoln County Tribune* that it cost "50c for men plus 5c federal tax and 18c for women plus 2c federal tax" to get into the decorated pavilion. The adjustment was reportedly needed "to eliminate book keeping due to the new federal regulations." (Courtesy of the Lincoln County Historical Society.)

"Elks Building," North Platte, Neb.

A structure with a long-standing presence in town, the Elks Building in North Platte had a history of dances for club membership taking place within its walls. The *North Platte Semi-Weekly Tribune* printed a story in 1919 about the Elks Building when it was the site of a particularly eventful "Elks' dancing party" at which a couple's car was stolen while parked outside. The vehicle was later located in Overton. (Author's collection.)

As in many other communities throughout the state, dances sometimes took place in Grant even without a building. Here, on Central Avenue in downtown Grant, festivals and street dances were frequently well attended and featured "old time dancing," particularly throughout the 1950s and 1960s. The *Tribune-Sentinel* reported in 1963 that a Friday night street dance in Grant was busy, but the one scheduled for Saturday was rained out. In true Nebraskan fashion, the dance attendees "were so glad to have the rain that there were few complaints." (Author's collection.)

The Duchess Hotel in Ogallala was a regular venue for events and activities, particularly those involving dances. In 1939, the *Keith County News* reported that the local Dinner-Dance club met at the Duchess Hotel for an evening party. Later in the week, "a dancing party" at the venue was in honor of "a group of college students home for the holidays." (Author's collection.)

The American Legion Hall in Ogallala has had a lengthy tenure as a dance venue. As far back as 1926, the *Keith County News* ran an advertisement for an "Old Time Dance" at the American Legion Hall. The space was also a frequent spot for the Oregon Trail Square Dance Club, which held a seasonal series of dances. (Author's collection.)

Sidney's Country Club was home to a number of monthly dances, coordinated and promoted tirelessly by a committee. Some of its advertisements in the *Sidney Telegraph* were for Grabill's Merry Makers and Hink Barker and his orchestra, two of the musical groups brought in to perform at the club's ballroom. A note in the *Sidney News* from 1927 found that all participants of a recent dance "enjoyed themselves immensely," making the committee's efforts worthwhile for the community. (Author's collection.)

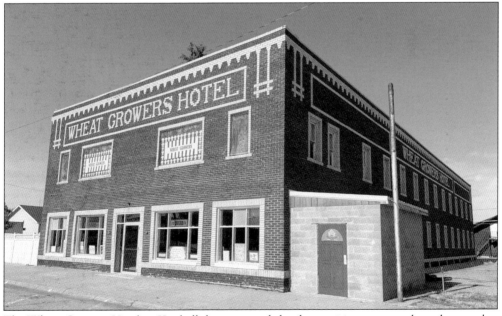

The Wheat Growers Hotel in Kimball demonstrated that larger cities were not the only ones that had space for dances. Performers such as Gayle's Musical Merrymakers of Lincoln and the Morris Orchestra provided music at the hotel, which held dances for both the general community and various specific occasions, including a farewell party for residents moving out of Kimball. (Author's collection.)

The Japanese Hall in Mitchell was also known as the Japanese American Hall. There was an additional Japanese Hall facility in Scottsbluff, and there are records of another in North Platte. These community buildings hosted dances, often centered around Japanese heritage specifically, as well as meals, singing, and other activities. (Courtesy of Legacy of the Plains–Japanese Hall in Gering, Nebraska.)

Sandford Hall in Mitchell is located on the Scotts Bluff County Fairgrounds. The *Star-Herald* noted that Sandford Hall was built in 1934 "with the help of local school boys . . . in a short three months." It replaced the Mitchell Dance Pavilion, which had been located at the same spot but burned down earlier that year. Now, the dance hall is the site of annual fair dances and is listed in the National Register of Historic Places. (Courtesy of Creative Commons.)

Located between Gering and Scottsbluff, Terrytown offered a dance facility of its own: Terry's Arena. Especially throughout the late 1950s and early 1960s, the arena hosted numerous dances and operated as a community center. In 1963, the *Scottsbluff Daily Star-Herald* announced that a Policeman's Ball to be held at Terry's Arena was postponed due to the assassination of Pres. John F. Kennedy, demonstrating that national events could impact even the smallest community's routines. (Courtesy of Legacy of the Plains in Gering, Nebraska.)

Terry's Arena in Terrytown was used for community activities other than dancing, such as roller skating, which often took place on Fridays. However, a notice in the *Scottsbluff Daily Star-Herald* on Christmas Eve in 1959 made it known that there would not be any skating the following day so a dance could be held instead. The Christmas night dance had music by the Foggy River Boys and ran until 1:00 a.m. (Courtesy of Legacy of the Plains in Gering, Nebraska.)

The Scottsbluff Country Club in Scottsbluff held dances within its clubhouse, and there are numerous records of a large annual dance held there for Halloween. It was reported by the *Scottsbluff Daily Star-Herald* that the 1923 Halloween dance was "the finest social event in the history of the year" and that the venue was decorated accordingly. To ensure the celebration attracted a large crowd, tables were arranged for games of cards to be played by those who did not want to dance. (Author's collection.)

The Lincoln Hotel Ballroom in Scottsbluff was one of three locations in the region to host a ball to celebrate Pres. Franklin D. Roosevelt's birthday in 1934. The American Legion Hall in Gering and Danceland in Scottsbluff were also host sites for the occasion, and all three dance halls expected to be packed full. (Courtesy of Legacy of the Plains in Gering, Nebraska.)

Japanese Hall in Scottsbluff, also known as Japanese American Hall, served as a community cultural center for generations, with the construction of the building being completed around 1926. While used primarily as a school to begin with, the hall became home to much more, including "*shibais*, or Japanese plays, and *odoris*, or Japanese dances." A *Star-Herald* interview with members in 1999 noted that the hall helped keep the Japanese American community connected. (Courtesy of Legacy of the Plains–Japanese Hall in Gering, Nebraska.)

The Phelan Opera House in Alliance, with street-side signage and the front entrance seen at the left here, was the site of cultural and entertainment events. This included dances, sometimes hosted by community groups, such as a 1911 occasion put together by the local Daughters of Isabella chapter. The *Alliance Times-Herald* promoted the dance as "the best of the season" and noted that residents "should not fail to attend" the event. (Author's collection.)

Colacino's Pavilion, east of Chadron, was originally known as Kelso's Pavilion. Dances were often held on-site, including many dinner dances, since the Colacino Supper Club building was also located on the property. In later years, the pavilion was painted pink and called the Pink Panther. Unfortunately, in 1985, the building's roof caved in, and the structure was razed. (Courtesy of the Colacino family via Larry Miller.)

The Sioux County Ag Society building in Harrison has had a variety of uses throughout its history. The building itself began as a livery barn around 1910 and then became a garage for a brief period before being remodeled into a dance facility. For several years, dances occurred nearly every Saturday night, which some older community members would attend just to spectate the dance and listen to the melodies played by the band. (Courtesy of the Sioux County Historical Society.)

BIBLIOGRAPHY

Jones, Patrick D., and Jared Leighton. *In Their Own Image: Artifacts from the Great Plains Black History Museum.* Brookfield, MO: Donning Company Publishers, 2014.

joslyncastle.com/about/the-castle.html

livingnewdeal.org/sites/community-center-dunning-ne

livingnewdeal.org/sites/tekamah-auditorium-tekamah-ne

mynehistory.com/items/show/393

Puschendorf, Bob. "Riverside Ballroom: A Personal Look at a Family Business." Norfolk, NE: Elkhorn Valley Museum Archives.

randymeisnerretrospective.com/2022/01/15/the-dynamics-from-scottsbluff

Street, Douglas O. "Band's Opera House, the Cultural Hub of Crete, 1877–1900." *Nebraska History* 60 (1979): 58–76.

usgennet.org/usa/ne/topic/ethnic/czechs/contents.html

Welsch, Roger L. "Nebraska's Round Barns." *Nebraska History* 51 (1970): 48–92.

www.brownell.edu/about-us/school-history

www.cityofhastings.org/parks/auditorium

www.fallscitynebraska.org/municipal-services/prichard-auditorium

www.hmdb.org/m.asp?m=179183

www.memories.ne.gov/

www.nps.gov/subjects/nationalregister/index.htm

www.starliteeventcenter.com/about

DISCOVER THOUSANDS OF LOCAL HISTORY BOOKS FEATURING MILLIONS OF VINTAGE IMAGES

Arcadia Publishing, the leading local history publisher in the United States, is committed to making history accessible and meaningful through publishing books that celebrate and preserve the heritage of America's people and places.

Find more books like this at
www.arcadiapublishing.com

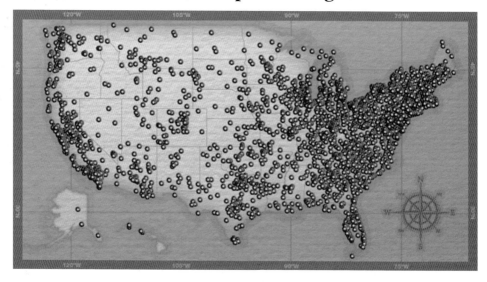

Search for your hometown history, your old stomping grounds, and even your favorite sports team.

Consistent with our mission to preserve history on a local level, this book was printed in South Carolina on American-made paper and manufactured entirely in the United States. Products carrying the accredited Forest Stewardship Council (FSC) label are printed on 100 percent FSC-certified paper.

MADE IN THE USA